CHAPTER APPROVED

GAMING IN THE 41ST MILLENNIUM

CONTENTS

PRODUCED BY GAMES WORKSHOP IN NOTTINGHAM

With thanks to the Mournival for their additional playtesting services

Games Workshop Ltd, Willow Rd, Lenton, Nottingham, NG7 2WS
games-workshop.com

INTRODUCTION

Chapter Approved is your passport to new gaming experiences in the 41st Millennium. Inside you'll find narrative-driven battles and scenarios depicting planetary invasions or brutal sieges, exciting new ways to play, mechanics for designing your own vehicles, and a host of new rules to take to the battlefield.

Amidst the thunder of guns and the clash of blades, the armies of the 41st Millennium go to war. Through tangled hive cities and continent-spanning manufactorums, sweltering death world jungles and crater-pocked wastes, forces of every sort clash in desperate battle. Invading armies rain from the heavens in fleets of drop-ships. Armoured spearheads smash headlong through enemy lines while insane warp storms rage overhead. Doughty defenders stand firm behind their barricades as seething xenos hordes swarm across the battlefield.

Just as the galaxy-spanning Imperium is a setting of near-infinite variation, so the battles that take place across its countless worlds are equally diverse. *Chapter Approved* provides a toolbox of rules and missions that can inject this variety into your games of Warhammer 40,000. Building upon the rich content already available in the *Warhammer 40,000* rulebook, *Chapter Approved* provides you with increased depth and choice, whether you prefer to play open, narrative or matched play games, or a mixture of all three.

OPEN PLAY: With open play, there are no limits to what models you can have in your army. Here we have included a collection of rules that take advantage of this most flexible of gaming formats. You can play an epic game of Apocalypse using every miniature in your collection, or field your converted models using our instructions on writing bespoke datasheets.

NARRATIVE PLAY: Here you will find missions that allow you to play out the story of an entire world embroiled in war, from the early stages of an invasion to the bloody battles that follow. These Planetstrike and Stronghold Assault missions can be linked together to create a campaign worthy of legend.

MATCHED PLAY: This section offers a wide range of exciting resources that you can use in your matched play games, including missions, Stratagems, Detachment abilities and more.

APPENDIX: Here we have collected updated points values, and rules for terrain, Battlezones and ladder campaigns. You will also find resources you can photocopy for use in your games.

> *To make full use of the contents in this book you will need a copy of the* Warhammer 40,000 *rulebook. To find out more about* Warhammer 40,000, *visit* warhammer40000.com.

WAYS TO PLAY WARHAMMER 40,000

Warhammer 40,000 offers three distinct styles of game for players to choose from, depending upon their preferences, the collections they have available, and what they want to get out of the game. These styles are open play, narrative play, and matched play, and each has its own strengths.

OPEN PLAY

For those who simply want to gather part or all of their miniatures collection, get it onto the tabletop and start rolling dice, open play is the perfect way to game. As its name would suggest, open play has few restrictions. Force sizes are not limited, and do not need to be in any way balanced against the army they are facing. Players are free to invent whatever storyline or framework for the battle they wish, whether that involves using the Only War mission provided in the core rules, or simply inventing their own scenario based upon the sort of game they feel like playing.

In this section of *Chapter Approved*, we present ways in which you can make your games of open play even more exciting. Starting with Apocalypse games (pg 8-21), it provides rules and missions for playing massive-scale battles of Warhammer 40,000 that involve every model in your collection. For such grand encounters, the flexibility of the open play format is ideal, allowing vast armies to rise and fall over the course of several hours or even days of gameplay. This section also provides instructions for writing bespoke

datasheets for converted Land Raiders (pg 22-29), with an easy-to-follow formula for creating tanks with any weapon loadout you like. You can also find ready-made datasheets for some examples we have made, and a blank template is available in the Appendix which you can photocopy and fill out for your games. Converting models is a great way to make your collection unique, as well as expanding your modelling skills, and open play is perfect for fielding such units, as there are no restrictions on the models you can bring to the tabletop.

These are just some examples of the kind of things you can do when playing open play games. Thanks to their sheer flexibility, open play games can be whatever you want them to be, from tank battles on hostile worlds to entrenched artillery duels, fights through darkened tunnel networks to desperate assassination missions and hunts for rampaging monsters. The only limits to open play gaming are the models in your collection, the gaming space you have available, and your imagination.

NARRATIVE PLAY

Games inspired, driven and regulated by a particular pre-generated storyline are usually known as narrative play battles. *Chapter Approved* provides a range of new content for use with this sort of gaming.

The first of these is Planetstrike (pg 32-43). This set of missions and rules allows players to fight out a full-scale planetary invasion, with attacking forces plummeting down from orbit to slaughter everything in their path. Will they sweep away the defenders in a tide of fire, or can the planet's garrison forces hold their ground and prevent their enemies from gaining a crucial foothold for the invasion to come?

The second is Stronghold Assault (pg 44-63). One side garrisons a string of towering fortifications, while their enemies charge forward en masse to smash down the walls or capture the defences for themselves.

Narrative play games are ideally suited to being linked together, the story and outcome of each battle impacting the next in ongoing campaigns that can last for weeks or months. Such personalised gaming is extremely satisfying, and generates war stories that will be retold amongst friends for years to come. The combination of Planetstrike and Stronghold Assault missions is perfect for this, depicting each stage of a blood-drenched war for an entire world.

MATCHED PLAY

Utilising points values and Battle-forged armies, matched play adds an element of competitive balance to games of Warhammer 40,000. In this section of *Chapter Approved*, you will find new missions to play – choose from Eternal War missions (pg 68-73), where both players compete to achieve the same objective, and Maelstrom of War missions (pg 74-79), where random Tactical Objectives can change the face of the game in a heartbeat. Both types of game are popular with players attending organised events such as tournaments, or playing 'pick-up games' against new opponents.

The new Faction-specific content (pg 88-99) later in this section list additional rules for a number of Factions that don't currently have a codex, including Warlord Traits, psychic powers and Relics. Battle-forged armies from these Factions also have access to the Stratagems and Abilities presented here.

Many matched play missions require you to secure objective markers, so rather than using dice or coins to represent them, why not go for something more original? In this section (pg 80-87) you will find tips on converting spare parts from Citadel Miniatures kits into eye-catching markers that are really worth fighting for.

AND MORE!

To make your games even more varied and exciting, you can use the rules provided in the Appendix. They work with any style of gaming; open, narrative and matched. The terrain rules (pg 102-105) represent some of the otherworldly landscapes in which your armies may have to fight. From deadly jungles to urban hive worlds, these rules are designed to complement your terrain collections. Meanwhile, Battlezone rules (pg 106-112) for industrial complexes and devastating warp storms provide new opportunities and challenges. You will also find tips on creating ladder campaigns (pg 114-115), which are ideal for generating an epic contest between multiple players. After this, we have included updated points values for a number of units that can be used in your points-based games, including some from the Forge World range (pg 116-123). Finally, you will find blank roster sheets and a blank Land Raider datasheet that you can photocopy.

OPEN PLAY

'The galaxy is a vast and terrible place, awash with a hungering darkness. Unto us alone does the Emperor give his light, that we might raise it high and drive back those ravenous shadows.'

- Chaplain Tellemorius of the Grey Knights Chapter

APOCALYPSE

Sometimes a battle will be fought that is so vast, so sprawling and spectacularly destructive, that it decides the fate of a world. When they are depicted upon the tabletop, such conflicts are known as Apocalypse battles.

Apocalypse battles are huge and dramatic tabletop conflicts, in which hundreds upon hundreds of infantry and squadron after squadron of fighting vehicles take to the field. The air darkens with waves of combat aircraft that rain fire from above. Titanic war engines grind across the battlefield, unleashing devastation with every volley, while space craft and artillery batteries annihilate their foes from afar.

Such grand conflicts have shaped the history of the 41st Millennium. Battles like the Fall of Cadia, the reclamation of Damnos, or the Doom of Valedor have seen the redemption or annihilation of entire worlds. Tales of incredible heroism and monstrous horror are woven from them, and the fate of whole star systems has been changed forever by their resolutions.

The rules for Apocalypse battles that you will find on the following pages

explain how you and your friends can play out these sorts of enormous engagements for yourselves. At its most basic, an Apocalypse battle is a game of Warhammer 40,000 that features two teams each comprising two or more players and using armies of substantial size on a larger than normal gaming table. Everything is scaled up for maximum carnage. For some, this is an opportunity to combine several smaller armies into one large force sufficient to play a game of this magnitude. For others – those who own massive armies and super-heavy war engines that rarely get to see the tabletop – Apocalypse is the perfect excuse to unleash these beasts upon their foes.

In battles of such size, the minutiae of exact game balance become far less relevant. Many Apocalypse games allow players to recycle entire formations of infantry or vehicles, or to hammer the battlefield with firepower from

titanic assets considered to be miles away from the action. In this way, Apocalypse is the ultimate expression of the open play mechanics.

More important to a game of Apocalypse is the mission you choose to play, as this will provide a simple narrative and a robust framework within which your game can take place. On the following pages you will find a selection of these, each one designed with clear objectives and an emphasis on gaming spectacle and fun, allowing you to engage in a clash of titanic proportions.

Probably the most vital part of an Apocalypse game, however, is how the players themselves approach the game. Assembling all of the miniatures and scenery required for a game of Apocalypse is quite an undertaking, and the largest games are likely to last for a couple of days' intensive gaming. Players need to work together within their teams to ensure that everyone enjoys themselves and gets to make the most of the huge forces they've brought along, and should be conscious that Apocalypse is not intended to be a fiercely competitive or finely balanced gaming experience. After all, in a setting where storms of firepower can decimate entire armies in seconds and war engines the size of hab-blocks bestride the battlefield, everything can change in the blink of an eye!

Apocalypse games should therefore be played for the spectacle, and the sheer joy of playing out such an epic encounter. Entire lances of Imperial Knights stride into battle, guns thundering. Armadas of Asuryani and Drukhari aircraft streak through the skies, ploughing bloody furrows through Tyranid super-swarms with their massed firepower. The greatest heroes of the 41st Millennium clash in numbers rarely seen to decide whether worlds live or die. For many players, the chance to visualise these kinds of iconic scenes is reason enough to play. Of course, having the opportunity to deploy every single model in your collection as part of a still-larger army, and to perpetrate the sort of wholesale slaughter that only Apocalypse provides, are also good reasons to get involved!

So read on, and whether your gaming group plans to besiege a hive city, evacuate vital dignitaries from a dying world, or stage the tank war to end all tank wars, over the following pages you will find all you need to fight out the largest and most catastrophically destructive game of Warhammer 40,000 you've ever seen…

UNLEASH THE APOCALYPSE

Apocalypse is designed to be played between two teams of players, where every player can field all of the miniatures in their collection. It's the ideal showcase for your biggest and best models – an arena where Titans duel across a corpse-strewn battlefield and super-heavy tank squadrons engage in deadly combat!

Setting up a game of Apocalypse requires a little more preparation than most games. Because of this, it's best to have a 'game organiser'. They will make sure all of the players know where and when to meet, decide on the scenario to be played, and set up the terrain for the battle.

Apocalyptic Armies and Sides

Apocalypse is played between two teams of players, or 'sides'. Whilst Apocalypse battles can be fought between just two players, they are especially suited to team play. The number of players in each side doesn't have to be the same, but it helps if neither side has more than one extra player than the other.

In Apocalypse, players can use any models from their collection. They can even use their entire collection if they wish! It's a good idea to split the players into sides in such a way that both teams have similarly powerful armies. You may wish to compare each army's Power Rating to determine this – ideally each side should have a Power Rating of at least 150. Each player in a side commands their own army, and all units on the same side are considered friendly towards each other.

Warlords and Warmasters

Before a game of Apocalypse begins, each player nominates one model to be his Warlord. As a result, there may be several Warlords on each side, each of whom will have a Warlord Trait, as normal. However, it is important to establish who is in overall control of each side, so the players need to agree on which of their Warlords is going to be the Warmaster for that game. The Warmaster is in overall control of whatever alliance or war effort is taking place. The player that controls the Warmaster gets precedence when players in the team disagree upon matters of overall strategy that directly affect more than one person in that side. Be warned, though – the head of the enemy's supreme commander is a trophy greatly prized by the foe…

An Apocalyptic Battlefield

Apocalypse battles require suitably large battlefields. The gaming area needs to be at least 6' by 4', and is typically much larger; we've heard of Apocalypse games being played on the floor, where the battlefield is 30' by 40'! Just as the players in each

side combine their miniatures into a single army, all of the players in an Apocalypse battle should combine their terrain collections together to ensure they have enough scenery for the battle. Don't worry if there are wide-open spaces though – in fact, these are quite desirable, as you'll soon fill the space with models!

The Time Limit

Instead of a turn limit, Apocalypse battles have a time limit, which is determined by the players or the game organiser before the battle.

Apocalypse games usually take the best part of a day to play, and therefore have a schedule to determine when the battle starts and ends. Typically, a battle will start at 9 or 10 a.m. and end at 7 or 8 p.m., though it is not uncommon for games to go on longer than this, or even to take place over two or more days. Because these games often overrun, the end time should be set at least thirty minutes before the game really needs to finish. In addition to start and end times, a number of breaks should be scheduled for players to stop for refreshments. These also serve as good points to bring reinforcements and reserves into the battle. When a break point is reached, complete the current battle round before stopping. This ensures both sides have had the same number of turns.

PICKING A MISSION & DEPLOYING

The players decide which mission to play (or devise one of their own). Each mission tells you how to set up the battlefield, how to deploy the armies, what special rules apply to the game, and how the winner is decided.

The three 'Apocalyptic War' missions at the end of this section are good for general games of Apocalypse, and represent the types of apocalyptic battle that have been fought many times over the millennia.

With the schedule set, the players gathered, and the terrain set up, it is time to begin the battle. Because Apocalypse is a team game, some time needs to be set aside for a group discussion of the strategy to be employed for the coming battle.

Once all of the commanders in a side are clear about their objectives and their strategy, the armies can deploy. This can take some time for Apocalypse-sized armies, and because of this there will often be a time limit for deploying each army – any models that are not deployed within this time start the battle in reserve, and can enter the battlefield as reinforcements during the next scheduled break.

TYPICAL ONE-DAY SCHEDULE

9:00am – Arrive and deploy
10:00am – Start 1st session
1:00pm – Lunch break
2:00pm – Start 2nd session
5:30pm – Dinner break
6:00pm – Start 3rd session
9:00pm – End battle

ORGANISING THE APOCALYPSE

The scale of a typical game of Apocalypse can make coordinating, recruiting and scheduling more of a challenge than for normal games of Warhammer 40,000. Here you will find some tips for organising large-scale games.

Game Organiser

We've already mentioned the importance of the game organiser, whose responsibility it is to ensure Apocalypse gaming sessions run smoothly. Most gaming groups find that assigning this job to just one person is much more effective than having a committee in charge, as a group of organisers may well spend as much time debating with each other how best to do things as they do organising the game. The ideal game organiser should be open to suggestions and advice from other players, but will ultimately make all of the decisions pertaining to how the game is run.

If you've taken on the mantle of game organiser for your group, there are four important factors you will need to consider.

'The Four P's'
- **People**
- **Place**
- **Playing Area**
- **Plan**

1. People

One of the first challenges you will encounter is the difficulty of getting lots of people in one place at the same time. This will never be easy, but it helps to be proactive. Instead of casually suggesting a game of Apocalypse, give your players a firm date, time and place. If you arrange the game far enough in advance for people to fit it into their schedules, you'll usually find that plenty of volunteers will be available. If there are a limited number of places then be clear on this right at the start, as trying to tell someone there isn't room for them later can lead to hurt feelings. Also, let your players know that if they can't attend a game

they've signed up for, they should let you know as soon as they can, as this will give you plenty of time to make other arrangements.

Large games can take quite a bit of time to set up and pack down, so it's a good idea to get a couple of players to agree to arrive early and leave late to help you with this.

Unfortunately, all this preparation doesn't ensure the day will unfold smoothly. People will turn up late, forget to bring things, and so on. As a game organiser, you should always be prepared. Bringing along some extra game aids and models yourself, and being flexible in re-organising which players are on what side is the key to success. Players that arrive late should join the game as 'reinforcements' during the next scheduled break. Those that have to leave early can hand over command of their troops to an ally, or withdraw their army by packing it away when they leave.

2. Place

You'll usually find that the place where you normally play games is perfectly suitable for games of Apocalypse too, but this won't

always be the case due to the scale of the battle. Local leisure centres, community centres and libraries often have function rooms that can be hired for a day or two. However, it's rare to find a venue that can be hired for free. Because of this, you should warn players that they may have to cover the cost of hiring the venue. Warhammer World in Nottingham, UK, is fully equipped to cater for large-scale games, and you can book tables in advance online.

Ensuring that the venue is right for everyone is important, and it's your responsibility to arrange transportation, if needed, to and from your chosen location. You should also make sure there are adequate facilities for refreshments on-site, or otherwise instruct players to bring plenty of food and drink with them.

3. Playing Area

Once you have an idea of how large a playing area will be needed, you must make sure that you have enough terrain for the battle. You don't need as much terrain in Apocalypse games per square foot of the table as you do normally, but you may still find that some more terrain is required. If this is the case, you should consider coordinating with your group to produce more. You'll probably find that the promise of a game of Apocalypse can act as a great spur for making extra terrain.

4. Plan

With the logistics of your game sorted out, you next need to make a plan for the battle. This should be written and sent to all players well in advance of the game. It should include information such as:

- Where and when to turn up in order to play the game. If you're organising a game that is going to take more than a day to play, then you will also need to include information about accommodation.
- A list of players and their contact details (a list of phone numbers is especially useful for tracking down missing players).
- What the players need to bring with them (armies, codexes, dice, tape measures, etc.).
- A rough value of the combined Power Rating of all the models each player will bring (asking each player to submit this well in advance is recommended).
- Spare glue – invaluable for any last-minute repairs!
- A schedule for the day stating when the game will start, when breaks will take place, etc, such as the one provided on page 11.
- A list of who will arrive early to help set up, and who will stay late to help pack away.
- What arrangements have been made for eating and drinking, or a note telling players to bring their own food.
- Any special or 'house' rules that will be used.
- An overview of the mission being played.
- Anything else you can think of that may be useful.

Most importantly of all, leave yourself fifteen minutes before the battle to explain the mission and any special rules you are using to all of the players that are taking part.

There is one final decision you will need to make, and that's whether to join in the battle yourself, or act as a neutral games master. This is a matter of personal preference, but we recommend joining in if you can, as by the time the game has started, almost all of the your work has been done. On the other hand, there are those who really enjoy acting as a games master in order to make sure that everybody has as good a time as possible. It also leaves them free to spring unexpected surprises during the game, such as unleashing sudden warp storms and cataclysmic orbital bombardments!

APOCALYPTIC WAR
RACE TO DESTRUCTION

Two armies to stumble across each other at an unexplored location. The first thing each will know of the other is when their breathless scouts report sighting the enemy. Whichever side is able to organise their attack the fastest will be able to grab the initiative and strike before their opponents are fully prepared.

THE ARMIES

The players and their armies are split into two sides as described on page 10. One Warlord on each side is nominated to be their force's Warmaster.

THE BATTLEFIELD

Create a battlefield using the deployment map below and then set up terrain as described on page 10. The players controlling the two Warmasters then roll off.

Starting with the winner, each side takes it in turns to set up an objective marker, until a total of six have been set up. These can be placed anywhere on the battlefield so long as the centre of each is more than 10" from the centre of any other, or from any battlefield edge.

DEPLOYMENT

Both sides secretly bid (and write down) the amount of time they want to take to deploy. Bids must be in whole minutes. The amount of time bid is the time that side will have to set up their forces on the battlefield. The side that bids lowest deploys first wholly within the deployment zone of their choice (in the case of a tie, the players controlling the two Warmasters roll off and the winner deploys first).

Once the first side has deployed, the opposing side does likewise in the opposite deployment zone, in the amount of time that they bid.

Models must be set up within their own deployment zone. Any units that are not deployed on the battlefield because there is no room or because the deployment time limit has run out, are placed in strategic reserves (see below). Note that this does not apply to units that are deployed using an ability that allows them to be set up elsewhere, such as 'Teleport Strike', 'Ambush', etc.

POWER LEVEL

Before battle begins, determine each side's Power Level by adding together the Power Ratings of all the units set up in that army. Whichever side has the lowest is the Underdog. If both sides have the same Power Level, the game organiser chooses which side is the Underdog.

FIRST TURN

The side that deployed first has the first turn.

STRATEGIC RESERVES

Any units not set up during deployment are placed in strategic reserves. These units can be set up on the battlefield during any of the game's scheduled breaks, but if they have not been set up by the end of the battle they count as destroyed, which may affect how many victory points your opponent scores.

When a unit arrives from strategic reserves and is set up during a scheduled break it is set up wholly within 6" of that side's battlefield edge (models that are larger than 6"

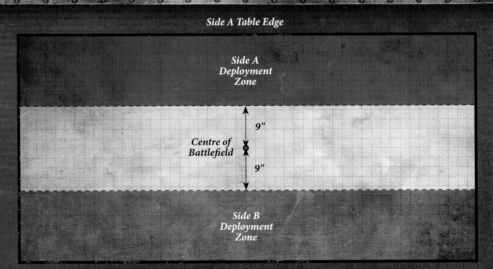

are instead set up so that they are touching their side's battlefield edge). If a unit cannot be placed because there is insufficient room, it must wait until the next scheduled break before arriving from strategic reserves.

BATTLE LENGTH

The battle continues until the time limit is reached, as described on page 11. Players should complete the current battle round and then end the battle.

VICTORY CONDITIONS

At the end of the game, the side who has scored the most victory points wins a major victory. If both sides have the same number of victory points, the Underdog side wins a minor victory. Victory points are achieved for the following:

Take and Hold: At the end of the battle, each objective marker is worth 1 victory point to the side that controls it. A side controls an objective marker if there are more models from their side within 3" of the centre of it than there are enemy models.

Slay the Warmaster: If the enemy Warmaster has been slain during the battle, the side that destroyed it scores 1 victory point.

Titanic Destruction: At the end of the battle, each side receives 1 victory point for each enemy TITANIC unit that has been destroyed.

APOCALYPTIC WAR
NIGHT MARCH

A battlefield is a confusing place, especially at night, when it is not uncommon for forces to be unsure of where other friendly forces are located, let alone the enemy! The resulting battle will find the two sides dangerously intermingled, with friends and foes scattered across the landscape in all directions.

THE ARMIES

The players and their armies are split into two sides as described on page 10. One Warlord on each side is nominated to be their force's Warmaster.

THE BATTLEFIELD

Create a battlefield that is at least 4' by 8' and then set up terrain as described on page 10. The players controlling the two Warmasters then roll off.

Starting with the winner, each side takes it in turns to set up an objective marker, until a total of six have been set up. These can be placed anywhere on the battlefield so long as the centre of each is more than 10" from the centre of any other, or from any battlefield edge.

The winner of the roll-off then chooses which long edge of the battlefield will be their battlefield edge. The opposite edge is their opponent's battlefield edge.

DEPLOYMENT

Starting with the side that placed the sixth objective marker, each side takes it in turns to set up a deployment marker, until a total of six have been set up. These must be placed on any battlefield edge, more than 48" away from the centre of any other deployment marker (as measured along the edge of the battlefield). An example of how this might work can be seen on the map below. Once all six deployment markers have been

set up, each side splits their force into three contingents, each roughly a third of the army. The players controlling the two Warmasters then roll off.

Starting with the winner, each side takes it in turns to set up one of their contingents wholly within 18" of one of their deployment markers (a different deployment marker must be used for each of the three contingents). Any units that are not deployed on the battlefield because there is no room are placed in strategic reserves (see below). Note that this does not apply to units that are deployed using an ability that allows them to be set up elsewhere, such as 'Teleport Strike', 'Ambush', etc.

Do not remove the deployment markers once all models have been set up – these show where strategic reserves may enter the battlefield.

POWER LEVEL

Before battle begins, determine each side's Power Level by adding together the Power Ratings of all the units set up in that army. Whichever side has the lowest is the Underdog. If both sides have the same Power Level, the game organiser chooses which side is the Underdog.

FIRST TURN

The players controlling the two Warmasters roll off and the winner has the first turn.

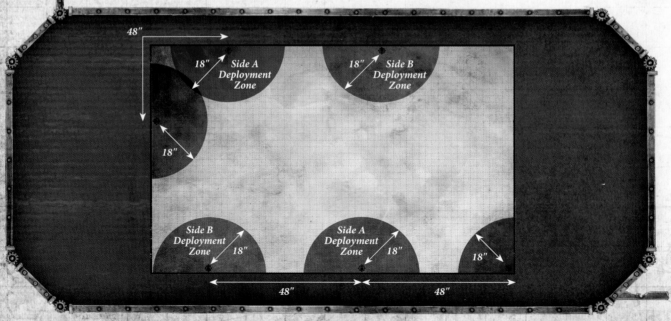

STRATEGIC RESERVES

Any units not set up during deployment are placed in strategic reserves. These units can be set up on the battlefield during any of the game's scheduled breaks, but if they have not been set up by the end of the battle they count as destroyed, which may affect how many victory points your opponent scores.

When a unit arrives from strategic reserves and is set up during a scheduled break it is set up wholly within 6" of that side's battlefield edge and wholly within 18" of one of that side's deployment markers (models that are larger than 6" are instead set up so that they are touching one of their side's deployment markers). If a unit cannot be placed because there is insufficient room, it must wait until the next scheduled break before arriving from strategic reserves.

ILL MET BY MOONLIGHT

During the first battle round, the maximum range of all shooting attacks and psychic powers is limited to 24". Targets that are further away cannot be seen or attacked.

BATTLE LENGTH

The battle continues until the time limit is reached, as described on page 11. Players should complete the current battle round and then end the battle.

VICTORY CONDITIONS

At the end of the game, the side who has scored the most victory points wins a major victory. If both sides have the same number of victory points, the Underdog side wins a minor victory. Victory points are achieved for the following:

Take and Hold: At the end of the battle, each objective marker is worth 1 victory point to the side that controls it. A side controls an objective marker if there are more models from their side within 3" of the centre of it than there are enemy models.

Slay the Warmaster: If the enemy Warmaster has been slain during the battle, you score 1 victory point.

Titanic Destruction: At the end of the battle, each side receives 1 victory point for each enemy TITANIC unit that has been destroyed.

APOCALYPTIC WAR
EXTERMINATUS!

Apocalyptic wars are terrifying affairs, and sometimes the combatants will unleash weapons of such vast power that they can destroy the planets on which they fight. The two armies have become so enraged that they care nothing for the consequence of their actions, even if it means their own destruction.

THE ARMIES

The players and their armies are split into two sides as described on page 10. One Warlord on each side is nominated to be their force's Warmaster.

THE BATTLEFIELD

Create a battlefield using the deployment map below and then set up terrain as described on page 10. The players controlling the two Warmasters then roll off.

Starting with the winner, each side takes it in turns to set up an objective marker, until a total of six have been set up. These can be placed anywhere on the battlefield so long as the centre of each is more than 10" from the centre of any other, or from any battlefield edge.

DEPLOYMENT

The side that placed the sixth objective marker chooses which deployment zone they want before deploying their entire army. The opposing side then does likewise in the opposite deployment zone.

Models must be set up wholly within their own deployment zone. Any units that are not deployed on the battlefield because there is no room are placed in strategic reserves (see below). Note that this does not apply to units that are deployed using an ability that allows them to be set up elsewhere, such as 'Teleport Strike', 'Ambush', etc.

POWER LEVEL

Before battle begins, determine each side's Power Level by adding together the Power Ratings of all the units set up in that army. Whichever side has the lowest is the Underdog. If both sides have the same Power Level, the game organiser chooses which side is the Underdog.

FIRST TURN

The side that deployed first has the first turn.

STRATEGIC RESERVES

Any units not set up during deployment are placed in strategic reserves. These units can be set up on the battlefield during any of the game's scheduled breaks, but if they have not been set up by the end of the battle they count as destroyed, which may affect how many victory points your opponent scores.

When a unit arrives from strategic reserves and is set up during a scheduled break it is set up in its side's deployment zone and wholly within 6" of the battlefield edge (models that are larger than 6" are instead set up so that they are touching a battlefield edge within their side's deployment zone). If a unit cannot be placed because there is insufficient room, it must wait until the next scheduled break before arriving from strategic reserves.

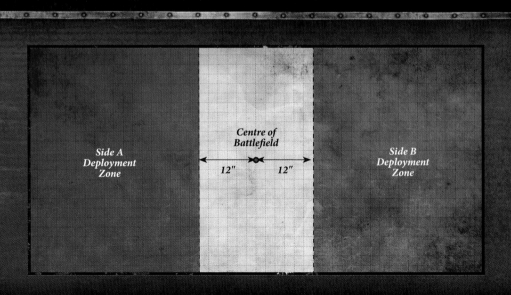

THE FINAL BATTLE

In this mission, units do not need to take Morale tests.

THE END OF THE WORLD

At the start of each battle round, the players controlling the two Warmasters roll off. The winner then rolls a D3 and adds the current battle round number to the result, before consulting the table below.

D3 + BATTLE ROUND	EFFECT
2-3	**Orbital Barrage:** Starting with the side that will have the next turn, each side selects a point on the battlefield and rolls a D6 for every unit within D6" of that point. Subtract 1 from the result if the unit being rolled for is a **CHARACTER**. On a 4+, the unit being rolled for suffers D3 mortal wounds.
4-5	**Virus Bomb:** Roll a D6 for each unit on the battlefield, with the exception of **VEHICLES**. Add 1 to the result if the unit has more than 10 models. On a 4+ that unit suffers D3 mortal wounds.
6+	**Cyclonic Explosion:** Every unit on the battlefield suffers D3 mortal wounds (units with more than 10 models instead suffer D6 mortal wounds).

BATTLE LENGTH

The battle continues until the time limit is reached, as described on page 11. Players should complete the current battle round and then end the battle.

VICTORY CONDITIONS

At the end of the game, the side who has scored the most victory points wins a major victory. If both sides have the same number of victory points, the Underdog side wins a minor victory. Victory points are achieved for the following:

Take and Hold: At the end of the battle, each objective marker is worth 1 victory point to the side that controls it. A side controls an objective marker if there are more models from their side within 3" of the centre of it than there are enemy models.

Slay the Warmaster: If the enemy Warmaster has been slain during the battle, you score 1 victory point.

Titanic Destruction: At the end of the battle, each side receives 1 victory point for each enemy **TITANIC** unit that has been destroyed.

BEYOND THE APOCALYPSE

These pages feature a number of battle themes and variant rules that can easily be incorporated into any Apocalypse battle. The aim is to allow players to expand the scope and depth of their Apocalypse games, and at the same time to make it straightforward for players to fight interesting battles based on the background and stories that are intrinsic to the 41st Millennium.

STORY-BASED OBJECTIVES

The missions presented on the previous pages are really just a starting point, and many players create their own missions for their Apocalypse games, based on a particular battle described in their favourite codex or Black Library novel, for example.

In many Apocalypse missions, victory is decided by which side controls objective markers. Objective markers represent key strategic locales or vital equipment – basically something worth the sacrifice of entire armies to capture. The missions on the previous pages all use objective markers as a method of determining the winner. For players who wish to base their games of Apocalypse on a narrative they have read or made up, these objective markers can represent anything they like, from a Mek-faktory that is churning out extra-armoured Stompas, to a warp rift from which legions of Greater Daemons are pouring forth. Usually this is done to tie the objective to the story, or because you want an especially impressive model or scenery piece to be the focus of the game. On pages 80-87, you will find an entire section devoted to the modelling and making of fantastic-looking objective markers for use in your games.

You can even create corresponding special rules to better represent your chosen scenario, such as the effects of a dangerous chemical leak in the vicinity of the faktory, or tides of Daemons that emerge from the warp rift at the start of each battle round. Such missions require more initial work, as the story, objectives and special rules have to be decided on and written out in advance, but the added level of immersion and depth will quickly make the effort worthwhile.

PERSONAL OBJECTIVES & SECRET ORDERS

Most games of Apocalypse are played between teams of players, and victory will either go to one side or the other. A variation on this idea is to give each player in a side their own personal objective. Overall victory is determined normally, but then the players in both sides can see how well they have done at achieving their personal objectives. The player in each side that has done the best is allowed to lord it over their teammates and claim the lion's share of the glory! This can lead to players doing all kinds of strange things and employing unusual tactics during a battle, often with very entertaining results.

As an example, you could say that each player must pick or randomly determine a personal objective from the following list:

- Control the most objective markers.

- Destroy the most enemy units.

- Control the centre of the battlefield with your Warlord.

- Kill the **Character** on the opposing side with the highest Power Rating.

- Destroy the unit on the opposing side with the highest Power Rating.

It's easy to come up with additional objectives based on the mission you are playing and the armies present. Each player then writes down their personal objective and reveals it at the end of the battle to claim their glory (or lack thereof!).

If you're the game organiser, you could alternatively write down 'secret orders' for each player, instead of allowing them to select a personal objective. Secret orders can be one of the objectives already described, or anything else you can devise. For example, you could say that a player must move a certain model to a certain point, or engineer a rival on their own side to be killed by the enemy, or advance their whole force into the opposing side's half of the table. Such secret orders would not be made known to the other players, creating some unpredictable behaviour!

THE UMPIRED BATTLE

Perhaps the ultimate form of Apocalypse is an umpired – or games-mastered – battle. In an umpired game, the game organiser forgoes the pleasure of taking part in the battle directly, and instead helps devise and adjudicate the game as the umpire, or games master. At its simplest level, this involves organising a game as described earlier, urging the players along to ensure the game moves at a brisk pace and sorting out any rule questions.

However, useful as these things are, an umpired game really shines when the umpire devises their own themed Apocalypse game, coming up with the story and background for the battle and any special rules that apply. We'd recommend only attempting this once you have a few games of Apocalypse under your belt and know what the players in your group like and, more importantly, what they don't like. Your aim should be to entertain your players, so they go away looking forward to the next game you organise. Because of this, it's worth putting some time and thought into the story you devise so that it feels convincing, and you may also want to make handouts for the players which you can give out at the start of the game. These handouts should explain the story, any special rules the player will need to know, and any secret information that only they have access to.

In play, the umpire can keep some pieces of information secret from some or all of the players. The umpire might, for example, decide that an area of what looks like clear terrain is actually dangerously radioactive, only revealing this information when an unwary unit enters the terrain. They could also unleash meteor showers on the battlefield mid-game, teleport alien forces to the front lines without warning, and all sorts of other fun surprises.

The unpredictability introduced by an umpire can make a game of Apocalypse even more immersive for the players, who will have to adapt on the fly to endure.

MULTI-TABLE GAMES

If you know a large group of players, at a games club for example, you can consider setting up a multi-table game of Apocalypse. You will probably need at least eight players to run such a game. As its name implies, a multi-table battle is played on several tables. A separate Apocalypse game is played on each, but the tables might represent different locations that are close to each other on a much larger battlefield, or different battlefields within a greater war zone.

Multi-table games are easy to organise, as long as you have enough space and players. All you need to do is set up two or more tables as you would for a normal game of Apocalypse, and then split the players so all tables have enough players. The same time limit applies to all of the tables. At the appointed time, all the games stop and all the victory points from all the tables are added together to see which side has won.

To add an extra level of immersion, you can theme the tables so they represent different types of battlefields, each with its own special rules and terrain. For example, one table might represent a large hive city full of towering buildings and sprawling ruins, another an ash waste, and a third an arctic ice plain. You can also link two or more tables together in some way, with a bridge, or some more esoteric means like a teleport array or a webway portal. Units on one table are allowed to move to the other table via that link. Alternatively, the events that take place on one table can affect another linked table. For example, one table could contain a vast siege cannon, while another could be 'the front' where the shelling is taking a devastating toll. One team of players is trying to weather the bombardment while their allies attempt to silence the big guns. The other side aims to shell their foe into oblivion, while receiving targeting data from their scouts behind enemy lines. Note that linked tables don't have to be physically linked in the real world, as long as players communicate what's happening on each one.

It's All About Having Fun!

The guidelines and ideas throughout this section can be mixed and matched by the game organiser to create the ideal battle. As with so many things about Apocalypse, the best way to decide which rules to use is to sit down and talk with your fellow players. Although the game organiser should always have the final say, there is little point in inflicting a set of rules upon a group of players that won't enjoy using them, so even the most dictatorial of organisers will find it helpful to talk through which special rules they plan to use and why. You'll find that a little bit of explanation is usually more than enough to get everybody onside and looking forward to the battle. As long as all the players keep in mind that the only really important rule is that everyone has a good time, then anything goes!

LAND RAIDERS

Throughout ten thousand years of warfare and turmoil, the Land Raider has remained amongst the mightiest and most iconic of all Imperial war machines. Whilst many follow a standard build pattern, there are those that have been modified for specific battle scenarios, their carefully calibrated weapons an orchestra of destruction.

Land Raiders are enormous battle tanks that rank amongst the mightiest war engines deployed by Space Marine Chapters and Chaos Space Marine warbands. These vehicles are exceptionally advanced, incorporating ancient technology understood only dimly – if at all – by most Tech-Priests of the Adeptus Mechanicus. Each Land Raider is inestimably valuable, for the secrets of their construction are now known only to a blessed few, and the resources required to construct even one such machine could produce a hundred lesser tanks.

Such effort and expenditure is justified as soon as the Land Raider rolls into battle. As the ground shudders beneath its tracks, the tank's formidable arsenal of weaponry wreaks havoc through the enemy ranks. Searing beams leap from its lascannons, converging on the enemy's heaviest war engines and punching through their armour to ignite ammunition stores and rupture power cells. At the same time, the Land Raider's twin heavy bolter howls, spitting streams of self-propelled, mass-reactive bolts that punch through armour and flesh to blow enemy infantry apart in welters of gore. When coupled with the thumping firepower of a pintle storm bolter or the fire-and-forget lethality of a hunter-killer missile, this ferocious battery of weapons can reduce entire enemy formations to blazing wreckage and heaped corpses in moments.

CONVERTING MODELS FOR OPEN PLAY GAMES

Many hobbyists enjoy the creative challenge of converting some or all of the models in their collection by customising them with parts taken from other Citadel Miniatures kits. You can convert models to tie them to a story you have read, or simply to make them stand out even more on the tabletop. The versatile Land Raider kit is a good candidate for this sort of thing. It has multiple weapon options, from its powerful hull-mounted gun to its customisable side-sponsons. Switching out the standard weapons allows you to create a whole range of tanks with various battlefield capabilities, each suited to a different kind of warfare. On the following pages you will find instructions for creating bespoke datasheets for converted Land Raiders, as well as a few examples for conversions we've made. Because these datasheets don't have a points value, they can't be used in matched play games, but they are ideal for open play games in which you can field any unit you like, from an Imperial tank bristling with lascannons, to a brutal Chaos monstrosity replete with an array of barbarous guns.

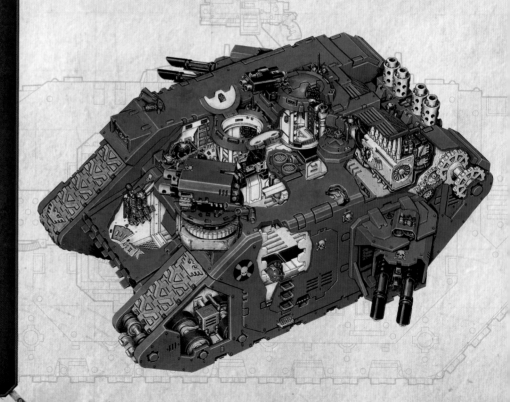

As valuable as its offensive capacity is the Land Raider's herculean resilience. Boasting monobonded adamantium armour sheathed in thermorepugnant ceramite plates, the Land Raider can shrug off cannon shells, laser blasts and the impact of monstrous talons without slowing. The tank's machine spirit is bellicose and formidable, allowing it to keep moving and firing even when its living crew are injured or incapacitated. Meanwhile its mechanical systems are multiply redundant and auto-sanctified, meaning that nothing short of the most ruinous damage can impact the Land Raider's combat effectiveness.

All this makes the Land Raider not only a potent and versatile battle tank, but also an exceptional infantry transport. With space in its troop bay to carry up to ten power-armoured battle-brothers or five Terminators, along with all of their ammunition and battle gear, the Land Raider can rapidly relocate a formidable force of super-human warriors in almost total safety. Smashing through enemy forces, shrugging off incoming fire and bulldozing ruins, barricades and undergrowth, the Land Raider delivers its living cargo, before lingering to support them with its devastating firepower.

Historically, Land Raiders were utilised during the era of the Great Crusade and the Horus Heresy to orchestrate massed Space Marine offensives. Hundreds of these titanic tanks rolled into battle, raising miles-high dust trails and shaking the very ground. Nothing could stand before their fury. Since those days, Land Raiders have grown scarcer, their strength spread thin across countless war zones. Forced to fulfil a wider variety of strategic roles, the core template of the Land Raider has been diversified through innovation and necessity. Certain widespread variants have arisen. The Land Raider Crusader, for example, was developed by the Black Templars for rapid armoured assaults on heavily defended enemy positions. Boasting an extended troop bay, a short-ranged but lethal multi-melta, and the withering anti-infantry firepower of hurricane bolter arrays, this belligerent engine excels at overrunning trench lines and barricades. The Land Raider Redeemer, by comparison, has been retrofitted for the horrific confines of urban warfare. Mounting a pair of immense flamestorm cannons, this vehicle can flood a stronghold or fortified ruin with cleansing fire and eradicate swathes of dug-in enemy infantry in moments.

There are rarer examples of variant Land Raiders, patterns that have been developed only by specific Space Marine Chapters and kept solely for their usage. Such innovation is frowned upon by the machine priests of the Adeptus Mechanicus, for within the bounds of the Imperium innovation is a heretical practice. Thus far, however, necessity has stayed the hand of the Adeptus Mechanicus, as it is impossible to deny the effectiveness of such variants in battle.

These specialist Land Raider variants are named by their creators, and influenced by the predilections of their patron Chapters. The tank-busting Terminus Ultra – developed by the Ultramarines – is the most common, and it has been adopted by various other Chapters. By comparison, the Mjalnar-pattern Land Raider of the Space Wolves mounts twin-linked helfrost cannons that can freeze their target in a heartbeat, while the flamestorm cannons and assault cannons of the Angel Infernus-pattern Land Raider of the Blood Angels help the transport excel against infantry at close range.

The Heretic Astartes possess their own Land Raiders, monstrous war engines baptised in blood and reeking of hate and malevolence. Some of these abominations are truly ancient, battle-tanks that levelled their guns against the battlements of the Emperor's palace during the final days of the Horus Heresy. Others are built upon daemonic forge planets within the bounds of the Cicatrix Maledictum, led into damnation when their Chapter turns renegade, or are stolen from defeated loyalists, their machine spirits tortured and broken to obedience by their new masters. Whatever their provenance, Chaos Space Marine Land Raiders are every bit as fearsome as their loyalist counterparts are noble. Their hulls bristle with metal spikes and leering gargoyles. Rattling chains dangle from their armour plates, threaded with the rune-carved skulls of slain foes and gory trophies taken from the field of battle. Eye-searing runes and daemonic sigils are blazoned across their hulls, and auras of unspeakable evil hang around them like shrouds.

Some of these fell war machines are marked by the Dark Gods, their hulls twisted like flesh into fanged maws and grasping limbs. They may dance with spectral soul-fires or be wreathed in choking clouds of droning plague flies. They may mount ferocious arrays of churning brazen blades to butcher the foe, or braziers from which billow fumes of a soporific, hallucinogenic nature. They may even bear sacrificial altars upon their broad backs, or play host to malevolent daemonic entities that lurk within them and direct their weaponry like parasites.

Just as some of the loyalist Space Marine Chapters have adapted their Land Raiders to suit their particular styles of warfare, so some especially well-resourced or innovative Heretic Astartes factions have done the same. Perhaps the most enduring traitor Land Raider variant so far recorded is the Hades Diabolus, which was developed by the Black Legion. Bristling with mid-to-long-range anti-infantry firepower, the Hades Diabolus can unleash a withering hurricane of shots that shred enemy infantry in seconds, and reduce artillery, walkers and even light tanks to sparking wreckage. This fearsome weapon has been encountered in several war zones around the sundered Cadian Gate, and its usage is spreading.

LAND RAIDER VARIANTS

On these pages we provide you with some guidelines on how to write open play datasheets for simple Land Raider conversions, as well as providing you with some examples that we have created ourselves.

Converting and modifying miniatures is an easy and exciting aspect of the Warhammer 40,000 hobby. With certain models, such as the Land Raider – which has weapon mountings and fittings that are interchangeable with several other Space Marine vehicles – it is straightforward to create an entirely new vehicle variant. It is just as simple to create a datasheet for these converted miniatures so that you can field them on the battlefield in open play games.

1. Select Primary Sponson Weapons

Start by selecting the primary sponson weapons for your Land Raider from the list below. This will also determine the vehicle's initial Transport Capacity (TC). In general, the more weapons you add, the less models the Land Raider will be capable of transporting:

- Two twin lascannons (TC = 10)
- Two hurricane bolters (**IMPERIUM** only, TC = 16)
- Two flamestorm cannons (**IMPERIUM** only, TC = 12)

2. Select Secondary Sponson Weapons

Next, select a pair of secondary sponson weapons (if any) for your Land Raider from the list below, and adjust the vehicle's Transport Capacity accordingly:

- Two lascannons (-5 TC)
- Two heavy bolters (-5 TC)
- Two heavy flamers (-5 TC)
- None (-0 TC)

3. Select Hull-mounted Weapons

Then, choose a hull-mounted weapon for your Land Raider from the list below, and adjust the vehicle's Transport Capacity once more:

- Twin lascannon (-5 TC)
- Twin heavy bolter (-0 TC)
- Twin assault cannon (**IMPERIUM** only, -0 TC)
- Twin helfrost cannon (**SPACE WOLVES** only, -5 TC)
- Reaper autocannon (**CHAOS** only, -0 TC)

4. Select Wargear Options

All **IMPERIUM** Land Raiders have the option to take a hunter-killer missile, storm bolter or multi-melta. All **CHAOS** Land Raiders have the option to take a havoc launcher and either a combi-bolter, combi-flamer, combi-melta or combi-plasma. None of these weapons affects the vehicle's TC.

5. Determine Final Transport Capacity

If your Land Raider has 0 TC or less, it cannot transport any models in battle. Otherwise, your Land Raider can transport that many models. The type of models your Land Raider can transport depends on whether it is **IMPERIUM** or **CHAOS**. Refer to the examples on pages 25-29, substituting the number of models the example Land Raider can carry with your model's TC.

6. List Abilities

Write down your Land Raider's abilities (all of the abilities mentioned below can be found on at least one of the example datasheets in this section).

- All Land Raiders have the Explodes and Smoke Launchers abilities.
- **IMPERIUM** Land Raiders have the Power of the Machine Spirit ability, and **CHAOS** Land Raiders have the Daemonic Machine Spirit ability.
- All Land Raiders equipped with 3 twin lascannons and/or 2 lascannons have the Power Overload ability.
- So long as it is not equipped with either lascannons or twin lascannons, an **IMPERIUM** Land Raider can have the Frag Assault Launchers ability.

7. List Profile

All Land Raiders have the same profile, as listed on any of the example datasheets that follow. All Land Raiders created using these guidelines have a Power Level of 30 and the Lord of War Battlefield Role.

8. Keywords

Write down your Land Raider's keywords:

- Imperium Land Raiders have the **IMPERIUM**, **ADEPTUS ASTARTES** and **<CHAPTER>** Faction keywords.
- Chaos Land Raiders have the **CHAOS**, **<MARK OF CHAOS>**, **HERETIC ASTARTES** and **<LEGION>** Faction keywords.
- All Land Raiders have the **VEHICLE** and **LAND RAIDER** keywords. Land Raiders with a transport capacity have the **TRANSPORT** keyword.
- Finally, create a name for your Land Raider (e.g. Terminus Maxima) to be its last keyword.

The **<CHAPTER>**, **<MARK OF CHAOS>** and **<LEGION>** keywords are described in the appropriate codex. Note that for **IMPERIUM** Land Raiders, you can also choose **BLOOD ANGELS**, **DARK ANGELS**, **SPACE WOLVES**, **GREY KNIGHTS** or **DEATHWATCH**.

TERMINUS ULTRA

NAME	M	WS	BS	S	T	W	A	Ld	Sv
Terminus Ultra	✱	6+	✱	8	8	16	✱	9	2+

DAMAGE

Some of this model's characteristics change as it suffers damage, as shown below:

REMAINING W	M	BS	A
9-16+	10"	3+	6
5-8	5"	4+	D6
1-4	3"	5+	1

A Terminus Ultra is a single model equipped with two lascannons and three twin lascannons.

WEAPON	RANGE	TYPE	S	AP	D	ABILITIES
Hunter-killer missile	48"	Heavy 1	8	-2	D6	This weapon can only be fired once per battle.
Lascannon	48"	Heavy 1	9	-3	D6	-
Multi-melta	24"	Heavy 1	8	-4	D6	If the target is within half range of this weapon, roll two dice when inflicting damage with it and discard the lowest result.
Storm bolter	24"	Rapid Fire 2	4	0	1	-
Twin lascannon	48"	Heavy 2	9	-3	D6	-

WARGEAR OPTIONS	• This model may take a hunter-killer missile. • This model may take a storm bolter. • This model may take a multi-melta.

ABILITIES	**Explodes:** If this model is reduced to 0 wounds, roll a D6 before removing it from the battlefield. On a 6 it explodes, and each unit within 6" suffers D6 mortal wounds. **Power of the Machine Spirit:** This model does not suffer the penalty to hit rolls for moving and firing Heavy weapons.	**Power Overload:** If you roll three or more hit rolls of 1 for this model's lascannons or twin lascannons in the same phase, it experiences a power overload and suffers 6 mortal wounds. **Smoke Launchers:** Once per game, instead of shooting any weapons in the Shooting phase, this model can use its smoke launchers; until your next Shooting phase your opponent must subtract 1 from all hit rolls for ranged weapons that target this vehicle.

FACTION KEYWORDS	IMPERIUM, ADEPTUS ASTARTES, <CHAPTER>

KEYWORDS	VEHICLE, LAND RAIDER, TERMINUS ULTRA

The Terminus Ultra is a ferocious tank-hunter, dominating every armoured engagement it rumbles into.

OPEN PLAY

30 POWER

WRATH OF MJALNAR

NAME	M	WS	BS	S	T	W	A	Ld	Sv
Wrath of Mjalnar	*	6+	*	8	8	16	*	9	2+

DAMAGE
Some of this model's characteristics change as it suffers damage, as shown below:

REMAINING W	M	BS	A
9-16+	10"	3+	6
5-8	5"	4+	D6
1-4	3"	5+	1

A Wrath of Mjalnar is a single model equipped with a twin helfrost cannon and two twin lascannons.

WEAPON	RANGE	TYPE	S	AP	D	ABILITIES
Hunter-killer missile	48"	Heavy 1	8	-2	D6	This weapon can only be fired once per battle.
Multi-melta	24"	Heavy 1	8	-4	D6	If the target is within half range of this weapon, roll two dice when inflicting damage with it and discard the lowest result.
Storm bolter	24"	Rapid Fire 2	4	0	1	-
Twin helfrost cannon						When attacking with this weapon, choose one of the profiles below. If a model suffers any unsaved wounds from this weapon but is not slain, roll a D6; on a 6, the target suffers a mortal wound.
- Dispersed beam	24"	Heavy 2D3	6	-2	1	-
- Focused beam	24"	Heavy 2	8	-4	D6	-
Twin lascannon	48"	Heavy 2	9	-3	D6	-

WARGEAR OPTIONS	• This model may take a hunter-killer missile. • This model may take a storm bolter. • This model may take a multi-melta.

ABILITIES	**Explodes:** If this model is reduced to 0 wounds, roll a D6 before removing it from the battlefield and before any embarked models disembark. On a 6 it explodes, and each unit within 6" suffers D6 mortal wounds. **Power of the Machine Spirit:** This model does not suffer the penalty to hit rolls for moving and firing Heavy weapons.	**Smoke Launchers:** Once per game, instead of shooting any weapons in the Shooting phase, this model can use its smoke launchers; until your next Shooting phase your opponent must subtract 1 from all hit rolls for ranged weapons that target this vehicle.

TRANSPORT	This model can transport 5 SPACE WOLVES INFANTRY models. Each JUMP PACK, TERMINATOR or WULFEN model takes the space of two other models. It cannot transport PRIMARIS models.

FACTION KEYWORDS	IMPERIUM, ADEPTUS ASTARTES, SPACE WOLVES

KEYWORDS	VEHICLE, TRANSPORT, LAND RAIDER, WRATH OF MJALNAR

OPEN PLAY

The Wrath of Mjalnar surges into the enemy lines, pouring helfrost and las-fire into the foe to their ruin.

ANGEL INFERNUS

DAMAGE
Some of this model's characteristics change as it suffers damage, as shown below:

REMAINING W	M	BS	A
9-16+	10"	3+	6
5-8	5"	4+	D6
1-4	3"	5+	1

NAME	M	WS	BS	S	T	W	A	Ld	Sv
Angel Infernus	*	6+	*	8	8	16	*	9	2+

An Angel Infernus is a single model equipped with a twin assault cannon, two heavy flamers and two flamestorm cannons.

WEAPON	RANGE	TYPE	S	AP	D	ABILITIES
Flamestorm cannon	8"	Heavy D6	6	-2	2	This weapon automatically hits its target.
Heavy flamer	8"	Heavy D6	5	-1	1	This weapon automatically hits its target.
Hunter-killer missile	48"	Heavy 1	8	-2	D6	This weapon can only be fired once per battle.
Multi-melta	24"	Heavy 1	8	-4	D6	If the target is within half range of this weapon, roll two dice when inflicting damage with it and discard the lowest result.
Storm bolter	24"	Rapid Fire 2	4	0	1	-
Twin assault cannon	24"	Heavy 12	6	-1	1	-

WARGEAR OPTIONS	• This model may take a hunter-killer missile. • This model may take a storm bolter. • This model may take a multi-melta.

ABILITIES	**Explodes:** If this model is reduced to 0 wounds, roll a D6 before removing it from the battlefield and before any embarked models disembark. On a 6 it explodes, and each unit within 6" suffers D6 mortal wounds. **Power of the Machine Spirit:** This model does not suffer the penalty to hit rolls for moving and firing Heavy weapons.	**Smoke Launchers:** Once per game, instead of shooting any weapons in the Shooting phase, this model can use its smoke launchers; until your next Shooting phase your opponent must subtract 1 from all hit rolls for ranged weapons that target this vehicle. **Frag Assault Launchers:** Roll a D6 each time this model finishes a charge move within 1" of an enemy unit; on a 4+ that unit suffers D3 mortal wounds.

TRANSPORT	This model can transport 7 **BLOOD ANGELS INFANTRY** models. Each **JUMP PACK** or **TERMINATOR** model takes the space of two other models. It cannot transport **PRIMARIS** models.

FACTION KEYWORDS	**IMPERIUM, ADEPTUS ASTARTES, BLOOD ANGELS**

KEYWORDS	**VEHICLE, TRANSPORT, LAND RAIDER, ANGEL INFERNUS**

The Angel Infernus unleashes firestorms so intense that even the most dug-in defenders are reduced to ashes in a heartbeat.

SOLEMNUS AGGRESSOR

NAME	M	WS	BS	S	T	W	A	Ld	Sv
Solemnus Aggressor	*	6+	*	8	8	16	*	9	2+

DAMAGE
Some of this model's characteristics change as it suffers damage, as shown below:

REMAINING W	M	BS	A
9-16+	10"	3+	6
5-8	5"	4+	D6
1-4	3"	5+	1

A Solemnus Aggressor is a single model equipped with a twin assault cannon, two heavy bolters and two hurricane bolters.

WEAPON	RANGE	TYPE	S	AP	D	ABILITIES
Heavy bolter	36"	Heavy 3	5	-1	1	-
Hunter-killer missile	48"	Heavy 1	8	-2	D6	This weapon can only be fired once per battle.
Hurricane bolter	24"	Rapid Fire 6	4	0	1	-
Multi-melta	24"	Heavy 1	8	-4	D6	If the target is within half range of this weapon, roll two dice when inflicting damage with it and discard the lowest result.
Storm bolter	24"	Rapid Fire 2	4	0	1	-
Twin assault cannon	24"	Heavy 12	6	-1	1	-

WARGEAR OPTIONS	• This model may take a hunter-killer missile. • This model may take a storm bolter. • This model may take a multi-melta.

ABILITIES	**Explodes:** If this model is reduced to 0 wounds, roll a D6 before removing it from the battlefield and before any embarked models disembark. On a 6 it explodes, and each unit within 6" suffers D6 mortal wounds. **Power of the Machine Spirit:** This model does not suffer the penalty to hit rolls for moving and firing Heavy weapons.	**Smoke Launchers:** Once per game, instead of shooting any weapons in the Shooting phase, this model can use its smoke launchers; until your next Shooting phase your opponent must subtract 1 from all hit rolls for ranged weapons that target this vehicle. **Frag Assault Launchers:** Roll a D6 each time this model finishes a charge move within 1" of an enemy unit; on a 4+ that unit suffers D3 mortal wounds.

TRANSPORT	This model can transport 11 **DARK ANGELS INFANTRY** models. Each **JUMP PACK** or **TERMINATOR** model takes the space of two other models. It cannot transport **PRIMARIS** models.
FACTION KEYWORDS	**IMPERIUM, ADEPTUS ASTARTES, DARK ANGELS**
KEYWORDS	**VEHICLE, TRANSPORT, LAND RAIDER, SOLEMNUS AGGRESSOR**

OPEN PLAY

So terrifying is the volume of fire generated by the Solemnus Aggressor that it can shatter an infantry advance in a single volley.

HADES DIABOLUS

DAMAGE

Some of this model's characteristics change as it suffers damage, as shown below:

REMAINING W	M	BS	A
9-16+	10"	3+	6
5-8	5"	4+	D6
1-4	3"	5+	1

NAME	M	WS	BS	S	T	W	A	Ld	Sv
Hades Diabolus	*	6+	*	8	8	16	*	9	2+

A Hades Diabolus is a single model equipped with a reaper autocannon, two heavy bolters and two twin lascannons.

WEAPON	RANGE	TYPE	S	AP	D	ABILITIES
Combi-bolter	24"	Rapid Fire 2	4	0	1	-
Combi-flamer		When attacking with this weapon, choose one or both of the profiles below. If you choose both, subtract 1 from all hit rolls for this weapon.				
- Boltgun	24"	Rapid Fire 1	4	0	1	-
- Flamer	8"	Assault D6	4	0	1	This weapon automatically hits its target.
Combi-melta		When attacking with this weapon, choose one or both of the profiles below. If you choose both, subtract 1 from all hit rolls for this weapon.				
- Boltgun	24"	Rapid Fire 1	4	0	1	-
- Meltagun	12"	Assault 1	8	-4	D6	If the target is within half range of this weapon, roll two dice when inflicting damage with it and discard the lowest result.
Combi-plasma		When attacking with this weapon, choose one or both of the profiles below. If you choose both, subtract 1 from all hit rolls for this weapon.				
- Boltgun	24"	Rapid Fire 1	4	0	1	-
- Plasma gun	24"	Rapid Fire 1	7	-3	1	This weapon can be supercharged by the bearer before firing. If they do so, increase the Strength and Damage of the weapon by 1 this turn. On any hit rolls of 1 when firing supercharge, the bearer is slain after all of the weapon's shots have been resolved.
Havoc launcher	48"	Heavy D6	5	0	1	-
Heavy bolter	36"	Heavy 3	5	-1	1	-
Reaper autocannon	36"	Heavy 4	7	-1	1	-
Twin lascannon	48"	Heavy 2	9	-3	D6	-

WARGEAR OPTIONS	• This model may take a havoc launcher. • This model may take a combi-bolter, combi-flamer, combi-melta or combi-plasma.
ABILITIES	**Explodes:** If this model is reduced to 0 wounds, roll a D6 before removing it from the battlefield and before any embarked models disembark. On a 6 it explodes, and each unit within 6" suffers D6 mortal wounds. **Daemonic Machine Spirit:** This model does not suffer the penalty to hit rolls for moving and firing Heavy weapons.	**Smoke Launchers:** Once per game, instead of shooting any weapons in the Shooting phase, this model can use its smoke launchers; until your next Shooting phase your opponent must subtract 1 from all hit rolls for ranged weapons that target this vehicle.
TRANSPORT	This model can transport 5 <Legion> Infantry models. Each Jump Pack or Terminator model takes the space of two other models and each Cult of Destruction model takes the space of three other models.
FACTION KEYWORDS	CHAOS, <MARK OF CHAOS>, HERETIC ASTARTES, <LEGION>
KEYWORDS	VEHICLE, TRANSPORT, LAND RAIDER, HADES DIABOLUS

OPEN PLAY

NARRATIVE PLAY

'THE SEDITIOUS AND THE
MALIGNANT CLAIM THAT
ACCOUNTS OF MYRIAD IMPERIAL
VICTORIES ARE HYPERBOLIC, THAT
SUCH GLORY CANNOT POSSIBLY
BE MANIFEST IN SO DARK A
TIME. BURN THESE DOUBTERS,
FOR THE GLORIES OF THE
EMPEROR'S SERVANTS TRANSCEND
MERE TRUTH.'

- Officio Didactus Directive VI

PLANETSTRIKE

In games of Planetstrike, armies battle to the death in a devastating planetary assault. Players take specific roles – one is the Attacker, attempting to wrest control of a planet, and the other is the Defender, who will do everything they can to defend it from invasion.

Planetary invasions are swift and terrible affairs, characterised by deafening bombardments, earth-shattering explosions and storms of defensive fire that set the skies alight.

Thousands of battle-hungry warriors plunge from on high, pouring from the drop-craft and low-orbiting spaceships that darken the atmosphere like void-borne leviathans. Megatonnes of ordnance hammer down upon the defenders waiting below, destroying fortifications and reducing swathes of soldiery to crater-strewn corpses. Attack craft weave through lattices of withering flak, strafing the foe or else being swatted from the sky as plummeting fireballs.

Stablights sweep the lowering clouds, hunting for incoming enemy craft. Their touch is certain death to any invader caught in their beams, and red-hot debris rains from the skies as batteries of anti aircraft guns take their toll. Gigantic landers plummet from the heavens, shaking the ground with their impact before disgorging yet more warriors into the merciless meat grinder as the planetary assault rumbles on.

Below the chaotic skies lies a war-torn landscape, chewed up and spat out by thunderous waves of orbital bombardments. From churned bedrock and blazing forests rise the ruined shells of once-proud buildings, amongst them inviolable strongholds that jut defiantly from the tortured earth. The defenders of these surviving strongpoints clutch their weapons and look to the skies, praying to whatever deities they hold dear that their fortress does not become their tomb.

It is within this nightmarish crucible of battle that true heroes are forged. Some are reaving destroyers who plunge from the stars to sow death and destruction.

Others are staunch gatekeepers, stoic heroes who stand firm amidst the death that rains from the skies, bellowing commands that bolster the courage of the outnumbered defenders. It is these heroes whose blades must inevitably clash, and whose battles to the death will ultimately decide the fate of entire worlds.

Planetstrike is a war on all fronts, in which the fate of an entire world will be decided. Will you play as the Defender, setting up formidable fortifications and spending your warriors' lives to repel the invaders? Or will you play as the Attacker, raining hellfire and damnation upon the foe before sending an army of your best troops to claim the smoking remains of their strongholds?

Whether you choose to tear the planet from your opponent's grasp or annihilate the invaders from the skies, the rules presented on the following pages will allow you to craft exciting narrative games based around these roles. Using the framework provided, you can play out a battle – or even a series of them – that depicts the key moments of the fight to invade or defend your chosen world. You can even name the planet and determine its geography – is it industrial, a hive world or a jungle? – and collect armies and terrain that are themed around the story you wish to tell.

PLAYING PLANETSTRIKE

Planetstrike is an expansion that incorporates planetary invasion missions into Warhammer 40,000. In these missions, one player takes the role of the Attacker, and their opponent the Defender. As a result, the missions presented in this expansion are designed primarily for narrative play, telling the story of a planet under siege.

Planetstrike missions supplement the Warhammer 40,000 core rules with additional abilities, Warlord Traits, Stratagems and Detachments that help to better reflect the forces and tactics deployed by armies during such a battle. These additional rules are described below.

PLANETSTRIKE MISSIONS

If you wish to play a Planetstrike battle, you should first select a mission from the table below. Alternatively, you can roll to randomly select which mission you will play.

PLANETSTRIKE	
D6	**MISSION**
1	**Planetfall**
2	**Desperate Assault**
3	**Seize and Destroy**
4	**Stranglehold**
5	**Forlorn Hope**
6	**Planetquake**

PLANETSTRIKE ARMIES

The players choose who is the Attacker and who is the Defender, then each selects a Battle-forged army. The Defender's army must include at least one Planetstrike Defender Detachment (pg 34) and at least one Fortification Network Detachment. We recommend the Defender includes lots of **BUILDINGS** to withstand the Attacker's onslaught. The Attacker's army, on the other hand, cannot include any Fortifications, and must include at least one Planetstrike Attacker Detachment (pg 34).

The Power Level of the Attacker's army should be greater than that of the Defender's. Note that the Power Rating of any of the Defender's Fortifications do not count when calculating their army's Power Level. The Defender can include as many Fortifications as they want, essentially for free!

As with any game that puts players in different roles, we recommend replaying these missions, but switching the Attacker and Defender around to give both the opportunity to test out a different set of tactics.

PLANETSTRIKE BATTLEFIELDS

See pages 42-43 for some examples of different ways to create a Planetstrike battlefield.

PLANETSTRIKE ABILITIES

Planetstrike missions use the following additional rules:

Firestorm

The planetary invasion is preceded by a fierce firestorm.

The Attacker makes a series of Firestorm attacks at the start of the first battle round, but before the first turn begins; each mission will specify how many are made. The Attacker first places six dice numbered 1 through 6 on the battlefield, anywhere more than 9" apart. For each Firestorm attack, roll one dice: every unit within 3" of the corresponding dice's location suffers D6 mortal wounds. **INFANTRY** units hit by a Firestorm attack can choose to go to ground before the damage is rolled; if they do, they only suffer D3 mortal wounds, but cannot do anything during their first turn. After Firestorm attacks have been resolved, the location dice are removed.

Planetary Assault

The invader's forces rain from the skies to assault those on the ground.

In Planetstrike missions, the Attacker's units are not set up on the battlefield during deployment and instead start the game in Reserve. **INFANTRY** units and units that can **FLY** start the game in orbit, whilst other units start the game in a landing zone, just off one edge of the battlefield.

The Attacker rolls a dice for each of their units still in Reserve at the end of each of their Movement phases (this is called a Reserve roll) – on a 3+ that unit arrives from Reserve. Note that if a unit placed in Reserve is embarked within a **TRANSPORT**, they will arrive when their transport does, not separately (if rolling, make a single roll for the transport and its embarked units).

If the unit arrives from orbit, place it anywhere on the battlefield that is more than 6" from any enemy model. If the unit arrives from a landing zone, place it wholly within 6" of the battlefield edge designated as the Attacker's landing zone – the mission itself will describe which battlefield edge this is.

WARLORD TRAITS AND DETACHMENTS

If you are playing a Planetstrike mission, you can use the following Warlord Traits and Detachments when choosing your army, depending on whether you are the Attacker or the Defender.

PLANETSTRIKE DEFENDER WARLORD TRAITS

D3	WARLORD TRAIT
1	**Lord of Ambush** You can re-roll hit rolls of 1 for friendly units within 6" of your Warlord if targeting an Attacking unit that arrived as reinforcements this turn.
2	**Protector of Worlds** You can re-roll failed Morale tests for friendly units whilst they are within 6" of your Warlord.
3	**Planetary Defender** You have one bonus Command Point – this can only be spent on a Planetstrike Stratagem.

PLANETSTRIKE ATTACKER WARLORD TRAITS

D3	WARLORD TRAIT
1	**Master of Timing** You can re-roll one failed Reserve roll each turn.
2	**Burner of Worlds** When you make Firestorm attacks, add 1 to the total number you can make.
3	**Planetary Attacker** You have one bonus Command Point – this can only be spent on a Planetstrike Stratagem.

PLANETSTRIKE ATTACKER DETACHMENT

HQ
2-3

Troops 0-6	Elites 3-9	Fast Attack 3-6	Heavy Support 0-2	Flyers 0-2

Dedicated Transports: May include 1 for each other choice.

Restrictions: All units must be from the same Faction.

Command Benefits: +5 Command Points (these 5 CPs can only be spent on Planetstrike Stratagems).

PLANETSTRIKE DEFENDER DETACHMENT

HQ
2-3

Troops 3-9	Elites 0-6	Fast Attack 0-3	Heavy Support 3-6	Flyers 0-2

Dedicated Transports: May include 1 for each other choice.

Restrictions: All units must be from the same Faction.

Command Benefits: +5 Command Points (these 5 CPs can only be spent on Planetstrike Stratagems).

STRATAGEMS

If you are playing a Planetstrike mission, you can use spend Command Points (CPs) to use the following Stratagems, depending on whether you are the Attacker or the Defender.

2CP SCORCHED SKIES
Planetstrike Attacker Stratagem
Use this Stratagem before resolving your Firestorm attacks. You make D3 additional Firestorm attacks.

1CP RAPID DROP ASSAULT
Planetstrike Attacker Stratagem
Use this Stratagem before making Reserve rolls at the end of your Movement phase. D3 units of your choice automatically arrive from Reserve.

2CP HEAVY DUTY DROP
Planetstrike Attacker Stratagem
Use this Stratagem during deployment. Select one of your units – that unit starts the game in orbit, even if it is not an INFANTRY unit or a unit that can FLY. If the unit is a TRANSPORT, units can start the battle embarked inside it as normal.

3CP GROUND OBSERVER
Planetstrike Attacker Stratagem
Use this Stratagem after rolling to see where a Firestorm attack will land. Add 1 to or subtract 1 from the result (treat a 0 as a 6, and treat a 7 as a 1).

3CP LASERBURN
Planetstrike Attacker Stratagem
Use this Stratagem after resolving your Firestorm attacks, before the location dice are removed. Roll two dice; if you roll a double, nothing happens. Otherwise, draw a straight line between the two Firestorm location dice shown by the dice rolled; each unit that the centre of this line passes over suffers D3 mortal wounds.

3CP PLANETQUAKE BOMB
Planetstrike Attacker Stratagem
Use this Stratagem after resolving your Firestorm attacks. Resolve one additional Firestorm attack; this attack is resolved in exactly the same way, but hits all units within 2D6" of the location dice.

2CP TARGETING JAMMERS
Planetstrike Defender Stratagem
Use this Stratagem before the Attacker resolves their Firestorm attacks. You can move one of the Firestorm location dice up to 2D6" in any direction.

1CP DROP ZONE DENIAL
Planetstrike Defender Stratagem
Use this Stratagem when playing a mission in which the Attacker chooses a battlefield edge to be their landing zone. Before they choose, select a battlefield edge – the Attacker cannot choose that battlefield edge to be their landing zone. You can only use this Stratagem once per battle.

2CP FORTIFIED STRONGHOLD
Planetstrike Defender Stratagem
Use this Stratagem before the Attacker resolves their Firestorm attacks. Select a single BUILDING on the battlefield. You can add 1 to any saving throws made for that building for the duration of the battle.

1CP FOXHOLES
Planetstrike Defender Stratagem
Use this Stratagem when one of your INFANTRY units is hit by a Firestorm attack. Halve the number of mortal wounds (rounding up) suffered by the unit.

2CP KRAK TRAPS
Planetstrike Defender Stratagem
Use this Stratagem when an enemy unit arrives from Reserve and is set up on the battlefield. Roll a D6 for each model in that unit – for each roll of 6, that unit suffers a mortal wound.

1CP DIRECTIONAL VOID SHIELDS
Planetstrike Defender Stratagem
Use this Stratagem before the Attacker resolves their Firestorm attacks. Select a single BUILDING on the battlefield. Roll a D6 each time that building suffers a mortal wound as a result of a Firestorm attack – on a 4+ that building does not lose a wound.

PLANETSTRIKE
PLANETFALL

Invading forces orbit above, raining fire upon the planet's inhabitants, their landing parties inbound to take for themselves any fortresses still standing. The defenders must weather the storm and repel the enemy, no matter the cost. The attackers must not rest until the world is theirs.

THE ARMIES

The players choose armies as described on page 33.

THE BATTLEFIELD

The Defender creates the battlefield; they start by setting up their Fortifications anywhere on the battlefield. They then set up all other terrain on the battlefield however they choose to create a defensive position. Once the Defender has created the battlefield, the Attacker chooses one battlefield edge to be their landing zone – this is where their non-orbital Reserve units will arrive from.

Next, the Defender places six objective markers. One objective marker may be placed inside each **BUILDING**. Any objective marker not placed in a building can be placed anywhere on the battlefield so long as the centre of each is more than 6" from the centre of any other objective marker, any building or any battlefield edge.

If a building containing an objective marker is destroyed during the game, the Defender must place the objective marker where the building used to be.

DEPLOYMENT

The Defender now sets up all of their units, anywhere on the battlefield. The Attacker's units do not start the game on the battlefield, but use the Planetary Assault rules described on page 33.

FIRESTORM ATTACKS

The Attacker rolls a D3 and adds 1 to the result for each Fortification that is on the battlefield (add 2 instead if the fortification is a **BUILDING**). The total is the number of Firestorm attacks (pg 33) that the Attacker makes.

FIRST TURN

The Attacker has the first turn.

BATTLE LENGTH

The game lasts for six battle rounds.

VICTORY CONDITIONS

At the end of the game, the player who has scored the most victory points is the winner. If both players have the same number of victory points, the game is a draw. Victory points are achieved for the following:

Storm and Defend: At the end of the game, each objective marker is worth 3 victory points to the player who controls it. A player controls an objective marker if they have more models within 3" of the centre of it than their opponent does. If an objective marker is within a **BUILDING**, count all the models within 3" of the building and all the models garrisoning it when determining who controls the objective marker.

Slay the Warlord: If the enemy Warlord has been slain during the battle, you score 1 victory point.

PLANETSTRIKE
DESPERATE ASSAULT

The attacking forces have taken heavy losses during their initial descent, and they have but a tenuous presence upon the planet's surface. The defenders must take this chance to rout the enemy from their drop site now, before the invaders can establish a permanent beachhead.

THE ARMIES

The players choose armies as described on page 33.

WRACK AND RUIN

The Attacker has three additional Command Points to use in this battle. These bonus Command Points can only be spent on Planetstrike Stratagems.

THE BATTLEFIELD

The Defender starts by selecting one of the long battlefield edges to be the Attacker's landing zone – this is where their non-orbital Reserve units will arrive from. The Defender then creates the battlefield; they start by setting up their Fortifications anywhere on the battlefield. They then set up all other terrain on the battlefield however they choose to create a defensive position, bearing in mind that they will know from which direction the Attacker's land-based forces will assault from.

The Attacker then places one objective marker anywhere within 18" of the middle of their landing zone edge. Next, the Defender places five objective markers. One objective marker may be placed inside each **Building**. Any objective marker not placed in a building can be placed anywhere on the battlefield so long as the centre of each is more than 6" from the centre of any other objective marker, any building or any battlefield edge.

If a building containing an objective marker is destroyed during the game, the Defender must place the objective marker where the building used to be.

DEPLOYMENT

The Defender now sets up all of their units, anywhere on the battlefield that is more than 18" from the middle of the Attacker's landing zone edge. Unlike other games of Planetstrike, the Attacker can start this battle with any number of their units already on the battlefield; after the Defender has finished setting up their units, the Attacker sets up any of their units wholly within 18" of the middle of their landing zone edge. This area is their beachhead. At least one of the Attacker's units must be set up within this beachhead. The rest of the Attacker's units do not start the game on the battlefield, but use the Planetary Assault rules to arrive as described on page 33.

FIRESTORM ATTACKS

The Attacker rolls a D3 and adds 1 to the result for each Fortification that is on the battlefield (add 2 instead if the fortification is a **Building**). The total is the number of Firestorm attacks that the Attacker makes (pg 33).

FIRST TURN

The Attacker has the first turn.

BEACHHEAD VANGUARD

For the duration of the battle, the Attacker does not need to take Morale tests for any of their units that start the battle within the beachhead zone – these units are utterly fearless.

BATTLE LENGTH

The Attacker rolls a D6 at the end of battle round 5; on a 3+, the game continues, otherwise the game ends. At the end of battle round 6, the Defender rolls a D6; this time the game continues on a 4+, otherwise it ends. The battle automatically ends at the end of battle round 7.

VICTORY CONDITIONS

At the end of the game, the player who has scored the most victory points is the winner. If both players have the same number of victory points, the game is a draw. Victory points are achieved for the following:

Storm and Defend: At the end of the game, each objective marker is worth 3 victory points to the player who controls it. A player controls an objective marker if they have more models within 3" of the centre of it than their opponent does. If an objective marker is within a **Building**, count all the models within 3" of the building and all the models garrisoning it when determining who controls the objective marker.

Slay the Warlord: If the enemy Warlord has been slain during the battle, you score 1 victory point.

PLANETSTRIKE
SEIZE AND DESTROY

Far from the bedlam of the front lines lies an emplacement of utmost importance – if the invaders capture it, their foes will find a coordinated defence almost impossible to achieve. The defenders must keep the attacking force at bay lest they gain control of this vital stronghold.

THE ARMIES

The players choose armies as described on page 33.

FORTIFIED POSITION

The Defender has three additional Command Points to use in this battle. These bonus Command points can only be spent on Planetstrike Stratagems.

THE BATTLEFIELD

The Defender creates the battlefield; they start by setting up one Fortification, ideally a **Building**, in the centre of the battlefield – this is the Vital Stronghold. The Defender then places all their other Fortifications anywhere on the battlefield. They then set up all other terrain on the battlefield however they choose to create a defensive position. Once the Defender has created the battlefield, the Attacker chooses one battlefield edge to be their landing zone – this is where their non-orbital Reserve units will arrive from.

Next, the Defender places four objective markers. One objective marker must be placed on the Vital Stronghold (it must be placed inside it, if it is a **Building**). One objective marker may be placed inside each other **Building**. Any objective marker not placed in a building can be placed anywhere on the battlefield so long as the centre of each is more than 6" from the centre of any other objective marker, any building or any battlefield edge.

If a building containing an objective marker is destroyed during the game, the Defender must place the objective marker where the building used to be.

DEPLOYMENT

The Defender now sets up all of their units, anywhere on the battlefield. The Attacker's units do not start the game on the battlefield, but use the Planetary Assault rules described on page 33.

FIRESTORM ATTACKS

Add together the Power Level of the Vital Stronghold and any units embarked within it, and divide the result by 10 (rounding up). Then add 1 to this number for each other Fortification that is on the battlefield. The total is the number of Firestorm attacks that the Attacker makes (pg 33).

FIRST TURN

The Attacker has the first turn.

VITAL GARRISON

The Defender does not need to take Morale tests for any of their units that are within 6" of the Vital Stronghold.

BATTLE LENGTH

The Attacker rolls a D6 at the end of battle round 5; on a 3+, the game continues, otherwise the game ends. At the end of battle round 6, the Defender rolls a D6; this time the game continues on a 4+, otherwise it ends. The battle automatically ends at the end of battle round 7.

VICTORY CONDITIONS

At the end of the game, the player who has scored the most victory points is the winner. If both players have the same number of victory points, the game is a draw. Victory points are achieved for the following:

Capture at all Costs: At the end of the game, the objective marker in the Vital Stronghold is worth 6 victory points to the player who controls it. Each other objective marker is worth 3 victory points to the player who controls it. A player controls an objective marker if they have more models within 3" of the centre of it than their opponent does. If an objective marker is within a **Building**, count all the models within 3" of the building and all the models garrisoning it when determining who controls the objective marker.

Slay the Warlord: If the enemy Warlord has been slain during the battle, you score 1 victory point.

PLANETSTRIKE
STRANGLEHOLD

Though the battle for the fate of the planet still rages fiercely, the invading conquest is reaching its culmination in one quadrant vital to the war effort. Victory on this battlefield could well end the war in a single blow, so the defenders must do whatever it takes to deny their enemy.

THE ARMIES

The players choose armies as described on page 33.

THE BATTLEFIELD

The Defender creates the battlefield; they start by setting up their Fortifications anywhere on the battlefield. They then set up all other terrain on the battlefield however they choose to create a defensive position. Once the Defender has created the battlefield, the Attacker chooses one battlefield edge to be their landing zone – this is where their non-orbital Reserve units will arrive from.

Next, the Defender places three objective markers. One objective marker may be placed inside each BUILDING. Any objective marker not placed in a building can be placed anywhere on the battlefield so long as the centre of each is more than 6" from the centre of any other objective marker, any building or any battlefield edge. If a building containing an objective marker is destroyed during the game, the Defender must place the objective marker where the building used to be.

DEPLOYMENT

The Defender now sets up all of their units, anywhere on the battlefield. The Attacker's units do not start the game on the battlefield, but use the Planetary Assault rules described on page 33.

FIRESTORM ATTACKS

The Attacker makes two Firestorm attacks for each Fortification that is on the battlefield (pg 33).

FIRST TURN

The Attacker has the first turn.

BACKS TO THE WALLS

The Defender can re-roll failed Morale tests for their units.

BATTLE LENGTH

The Attacker rolls a D6 at the end of battle round 5; on a 3+, the game continues, otherwise the game ends. At the end of battle round 6, the Defender rolls a D6; this time the game continues on a 4+, otherwise it ends. The battle automatically ends at the end of battle round 7.

VICTORY CONDITIONS

At the end of the game, the player who has scored the most victory points is the winner. If both players have the same number of victory points, the game is a draw. Victory points are achieved for the following:

Storm and Defend: At the end of the game, each objective marker is worth 3 victory points to the player who controls it. A player controls an objective marker if they have more models within 3" of the centre of it than their opponent does. If an objective marker is within a BUILDING, count all the models within 3" of the building and all the models garrisoning it when determining who controls the objective marker.

Slay the Warlord: If the enemy Warlord has been slain during the battle, you score 1 victory point.

STRATAGEMS

In this mission, players can use Command Points (CPs) to use the following bonus Stratagems:

1CP DEMOLITION CREW
Planetstrike Attacker Stratagem

Use this Stratagem before one of your units fights in the Fight phase. For each wound roll of 6+ you make for that unit when it attacks a BUILDING that phase, the building suffers a mortal wound in addition to any other damage.

1CP DENIAL
Planetstrike Defender Stratagem

Use this Stratagem at any time. Select a single BUILDING on the battlefield. That building is immediately destroyed. If you would then roll to see if it explodes, there is no need to roll; the building automatically explodes.

PLANETSTRIKE
FORLORN HOPE

As a sign of the importance of this great assault, the invader's Supreme Warlord has entrusted his personal banner to his chosen warriors, ordering them to plant the standard atop the burning ruins of the enemy's fortifications. If the assault fails the banner will be lost, and with it, the battle.

THE ARMIES

The players choose armies as described on page 33.

THE BATTLEFIELD

The Defender creates the battlefield; they start by setting up their Fortifications anywhere on the battlefield. They then set up all other terrain on the battlefield however they choose to create a defensive position. Once the Defender has created the battlefield, the Attacker chooses one battlefield edge to be their landing zone – this is where their non-orbital Reserve units will arrive from.

Next, the Defender places three objective markers. One objective marker may be placed inside each **Building**. Any objective marker not placed in a building can be placed anywhere on the battlefield so long as the centre of each is more than 6" from the centre of any other objective marker, any building or any battlefield edge. If a building containing an objective marker is destroyed during the game, the Defender must place the objective marker where the building used to be.

DEPLOYMENT

The Defender now sets up all of their units, anywhere on the battlefield. The Attacker's units do not start the game on the battlefield, but use the Planetary Assault rules described on page 33.

FIRESTORM ATTACKS

The Attacker rolls a D3 and adds 1 to the result for each Fortification that is on the battlefield (add 2 instead if the fortification is a **Building**). The total is the number of Firestorm attacks that the Attacker makes (pg 33).

THE SUPREME WARLORD'S BANNER

At the start of the battle, before the first battle round begins, the Attacker must nominate one of their **Infantry** models to be the Supreme Warlord's banner bearer (use a marker to denote this).

The banner bearer cannot embark in a **Transport**, leave the battlefield, or move further than 9" in any single phase for any reason. If the banner bearer is a **Character**, they may be targeted by shooting attacks even if they are not the closest enemy unit (the banner makes them an easy target to enemy snipers).

If the banner bearer is slain, the banner is dropped; place the marker where the slain model was standing. Any other **Infantry** model can then pick it up by moving into contact with it. From that point, the banner remains with the new banner bearer, until they are slain and it is dropped again.

A unit automatically passes Morale tests if one of its models is carrying the banner.

FIRST TURN

The Attacker has the first turn.

PLANT THE BANNER

If, at the end of any turn, the Attacker controls an objective marker (as described in Storm and Defend, opposite) and the banner bearer is within 3" of the centre of that objective marker (if it is within a **Building**, they need only be within 3" of that building), they can plant the banner. If the banner bearer is slain while the banner is planted, it still counts as being planted until it is picked up by another **Infantry** model as described above. If it is picked up by a model from the Attacker's army, it remains planted. If it is picked up by a model from the Defender's army, it is cast down.

BATTLE LENGTH

The game lasts for six battle rounds. However, from the third battle round onwards, the battle can end earlier. If, at the end of a battle round, the banner has been planted for two consecutive battle rounds (including the current one), the game ends. This means that if the banner is planted, the Defender gets two turns to try and cast it down.

VICTORY CONDITIONS

Look to the Colours: At the end of the battle, the Attacker wins if the banner is planted, and the Defender wins if the banner is being carried by a model from their army. Any other result is a draw.

Designer's Note: *Obviously not all armies make use of banners as such, so players are encouraged to imagine what their army might use to signal victory. Necrons might erect some transdimensional relay, while Tyranids might plant a brain-like hive node, for example.*

PLANETSTRIKE
PLANETQUAKE

The skies glow with fire as a punishing bombardment rains down, and the shattered earth begins to crumble and break apart under the massive forces wreaked upon it. The battlefield is utterly consumed by war. Can the defenders hold fast as their fortifications crumble around them?

THE ARMIES

The players choose armies as described on page 33.

THE BATTLEFIELD

The Defender creates the battlefield; they start by setting up their Fortifications anywhere on the battlefield. They then set up all other terrain on the battlefield however they choose to create a defensive position. Once the Defender has created the battlefield, the Attacker chooses one battlefield edge to be their landing zone – this is where their non-orbital Reserve units will arrive from.

Next, the Defender places six objective markers. One objective marker may be placed inside each **Building**. Any objective marker not placed in a building can be placed anywhere on the battlefield so long as the centre of each is more than 6" from the centre of any other objective marker, any building or any battlefield edge. If a building containing an objective marker is destroyed during the game, the Defender must place the objective marker where the building used to be.

DEPLOYMENT

The Defender now sets up all of their units, anywhere on the battlefield. The Attacker's units do not start the game on the battlefield, but use the Planetary Assault rules described on page 33.

FIRESTORM ATTACKS

The Attacker rolls a D6 and adds 1 to the result for each Fortification that is on the battlefield (add 2 instead if the fortification is a **Building**). The total is the number of Firestorm attacks that the Attacker makes (pg 33).

FIRST TURN

The Attacker has the first turn.

DESPERATE TIMES, DESPERATE MEASURES

The Defender gains D3 bonus Command Points at the start of each of their turns.

SHELLSTORM

At the start of the second battle round, and at the start of each battle round thereafter, the Attacker resolves D6 Firestorm attacks. The location dice numbered 1-3 are placed normally by the Attacker (pg 33), then the Defender places dice 4-6 following the same rules. When all the location dice have been placed, the Attacker

rolls to see where each Firestorm lands, then resolves any damage.

TECTONIC UPHEAVAL

At the start of the third battle round, and at the start of each battle round thereafter, the Attacker rolls a D6 for each **Building** and consults the table below:

D6	RESULT
1-3	**Ominous Rumblings:** No adverse effects.
4	**Ker-rack!:** The building being rolled for suffers a mortal wound.
5	**Cave In:** The building being rolled for suffers D3 mortal wounds. Any units inside must immediately disembark. No unit can embark inside the building for the rest of the battle.
6	**She's Coming Apart:** As for 'Cave In' except that the building suffers D6 mortal wounds.

BATTLE LENGTH

The Attacker rolls a D6 at the end of battle round 5; on a 3+, the game continues, otherwise the game ends. At the end of battle round 6, the Defender rolls a D6; this time the game continues on a 4+, otherwise it ends. The battle automatically ends at the end of battle round 7.

VICTORY CONDITIONS

At the end of the game, the player who has scored the most victory points is the winner. If both players have the same number of victory points, the game is a draw. Victory points are achieved for the following:

Storm and Defend: At the end of the game, each objective marker is worth 3 victory points to the player who controls it. A player controls an objective marker if they have more models within 3" of the centre of it than their opponent does. If an objective marker is within a **Building**, count all the models within 3" of the building and all the models garrisoning it when determining who controls the objective marker.

Slay the Warlord: If the enemy Warlord has been slain during the battle, you score 1 victory point.

PLANETSTRIKE DEPLOYMENTS

These battlefields shown here are just a few examples of classic Planetstrike set-ups the Defender can refer to when creating their battlefield.

1. All-round Defence

The Defender has placed their Fortifications to protect the centre of the battlefield so that, whichever direction the Attacker comes from, they will be ready.

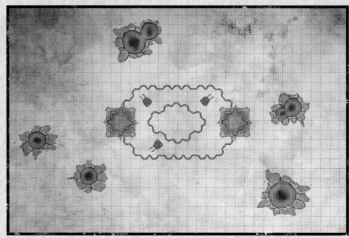

1. ALL-ROUND DEFENCE

2. Central Stronghold

This set-up is particularly useful in missions like Seize and Destroy, where the Defender places their best Fortification in the centre of the battlefield. Here, the central stronghold is guarded on all approaches by other sets of Fortifications, forming an outer perimeter of defences that the Attacker must fight their way through before attacking the vital target.

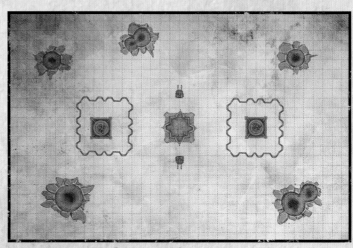

2. CENTRAL STRONGHOLD

3. Fortified Flank

This set-up is only recommended if the Defender is using the Drop Zone Denial Stratagem (pg 35). As the Attacker can't select the battlefield edge you choose to be their landing zone edge, the Defender can concentrate their Fortifications on that edge – be wary though, the Attacker's army could still come on from one of the two short edges of the battlefield.

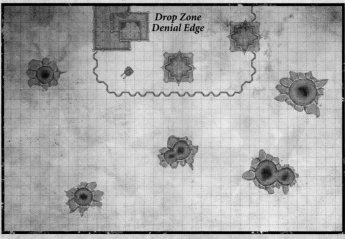

3. FORTIFIED FLANK

4. Kill-zone

This set-up is only useful in the Desperate Assault mission, where you always know which battlefield edge will be the Attacker's landing zone edge, and where the Attacker's starting forces may deploy. The Defender can then set up their Fortifications so that they surround the Attacker's beachhead zone and hence create a kill-zone with overlapping fields of fire.

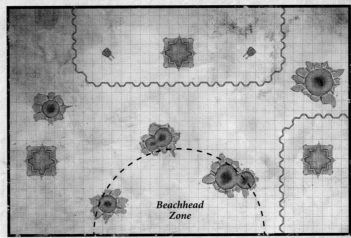

4. KILL-ZONE

5. Spread-out Defence

The Defender has placed their Fortifications all over the battlefield. Whilst it means that each Fortification is more vulnerable to attack, it prevents the Attacker from concentrating their Firestorm attacks and their forces on one part of the battlefield in order to wrest control from you and dominate the battle.

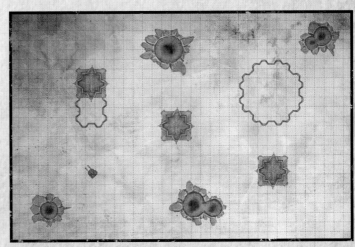

5. SPREAD OUT DEFENCE

6. Sacrificial Outpost

In this set-up, the Defender has placed two heavily defended bastions in opposing corners of the battlefield, with a series of defence lines between them. Whilst the Attacker can overwhelm one of them relatively easily by choosing a landing zone adjacent, capturing the other will prove exceptionally difficult, as they will have to cross the entire battlefield of defences to do so.

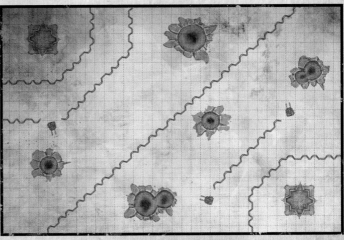

6. SACRIFICIAL OUTPOST

STRONGHOLD ASSAULT

In games of Stronghold Assault, two forces vie for control of a fortified war zone. Players take specific roles – one is the Attacker, determined to capture or destroy their foe's vital bastions, and the other is the Defender, who must dig in behind the fortress walls and repel the invaders with overwhelming firepower.

The galaxy's battlefields are punctuated with monolithic strongholds that reach towards the heavens. These fortifications are monuments to the unyielding nature of siege warfare. Many have endured centuries of unrelenting battle. Some have withstood more than ten millennia of grinding war, sheltering troops as they unleash their fury against the foe.

Built into the grandest bastions are weapons of such terrible magnitude that they can annihilate a battleship in low orbit. Such structures form the beating hearts of defence lines and trench networks that protect and connect whole webworks of bunkers and redoubts.

From sprawling greenskin scrapforts the size of cities to Imperial fortress worlds that watch over entire regions of space, these bastions are as varied as they are numerous. Some, such as nightmarish Medrengard, proud Solaxis or lost and lamented Cadia, are names known the length and breadth of the galaxy. Others – like Catachan with its living bulwarks of carnivorous jungle, or Fenris, home to the mighty Fang – are famed for their more unconventional defences.

Yet even the most formidable series of fortifications are naught but walls and barricades without a garrison to defend them. Only when soldiers man battlements and operate weapon systems is a fortress' true defensive potential realised. A single squad of warriors can prove themselves the equal of hundreds when occupying a bunker, pouring firepower into their enemies with impunity, safe from all but the most punishing retaliation.

It is no surprise, then, that the key to victory in any theatre of war is often to seize control of its fortifications. Commanding such assets allows supply lines to be safeguarded, entire regions to be denied to the foe, and massive enemy offensives to be weathered against the odds. So precious are these fortified networks that commanders will spend countless lives to wrest them from their foes.

In such a dark era, the death toll required for victory is rarely a consideration, however. Determined to succeed, commanders hurl their warriors against the enemy's walls and guns in their hundreds. Sappers and demolition experts charge forwards, pelting through hails of fire to slap explosive charges onto bulkheads and hatches. Artillery pieces and battle tanks elevate their barrels and spit their shells in looping arcs to come crashing down upon armoured structures until they tumble in flaming ruin. Aircraft sweep overhead, raining bombs upon trenches and ramparts to fill them with fire.

Many commanders also have access to more insidious or esoteric weapons of siege warfare. Tunnelling warheads churn through bedrock to detonate amidst reinforced foundations. Powerful psykers flay the defenders' minds, fortress walls no protection against the razored talons of the warp. Xenos warrior constructs phase out of synch with reality, passing through bunker doors and bulwarks like ghosts before solidifying again to wreak havoc within. Towering monsters and abhorrent daemons rampage forward, shrugging off

the defenders' fire before tearing down their strongholds with sheer brute force.

For all this devastation and horror, the victors in such grinding siege warfare are most often those with the willpower to prevail. Such heroes overcome their foes no matter the cost, and survive to raise their colours over fortifications strewn with the mangled remains of the enemy dead.

The rules on the pages that follow give you everything you need to play your own Stronghold Assault games. Taking the roles of Attacker and Defender, you can play out your own exciting narratives, or even link together several games to depict the key moments in the besiegement of a larger fortress.

You can even play out a campaign of planetary invasion by combining a series of Planetstrike missions (pg 36-41) with those from this section to determine the fate of an entire planet. From the moment enemy ships appear in orbit to the desperate battles in the ruins, from the initial surge of the attacking forces to the courageous last stand of the defenders behind their walls, such a campaign follows an invasion through from inception to glorious victory or bloody defeat.

PLAYING STRONGHOLD ASSAULT

Stronghold Assault is an expansion that incorporates siege-themed missions into Warhammer 40,000. In these missions, one player takes the role of the Attacker, and their opponent the Defender. As a result, the missions presented in this expansion are designed primarily for narrative play, telling the story of a fortress under siege.

Stronghold Assault missions supplement the Warhammer 40,000 core rules with additional abilities, Warlord Traits, Stratagems and Detachments that help to better reflect the forces and tactics deployed by armies during such a battle. These additional rules are described below.

STRONGHOLD ASSAULT MISSIONS

If you wish to play a Stronghold Assault battle, you should first select a mission from the table below. Alternatively, you can roll to randomly select which mission you will play.

STRONGHOLD ASSAULT	
D6	**MISSION**
1	Breakthrough
2	Bunker Assault
3	All-out Attack
4	Crossfire
5	The Big Push
6	Last Stand

STRONGHOLD ASSAULT ARMIES

The players choose who is the Attacker and who is the Defender, then each selects a Battle-forged army. The Defender's army must include at least one Fortification Network Detachment or one Stronghold Assault Defender Detachment (pg 46). At least one of the Defender's Fortifications must be a **BUILDING** (pg 57-63). The Attacker's army must include at least one Stronghold Assault Attacker Detachment (pg 46), and the Power Level of the Attacker's army should be more than the Defender's.

As with any game that puts players in different roles, we recommend replaying these missions, but switching the Attacker and Defender around to give both the opportunity to test out a different set of tactics.

*Designer's Note: In the Breakthrough and Crossfire missions the Attacker must attempt to move off the Defender's battlefield edge. We find that these missions are more rewarding with ground-based armies that contain few, if any, units that can **FLY**.*

STRONGHOLD ASSAULT ABILITIES

Stronghold Assault missions use the following additional rules:

Big Guns Never Tire

The invaders have brought along their heaviest ordnance to level the defences of the foe.

The Attacker's models can move and shoot Heavy weapons without incurring the -1 penalty to their hit rolls, but only when targeting a **BUILDING**.

Demolitions

The attacking troops are equipped with demolition tools and explosive charges to breach the enemy's defences.

Each time the Attacker makes a wound roll of 6+ for a model attacking a **BUILDING** in the Fight phase, the building suffers a mortal wound in addition to any other damage.

Hold at All Costs

The defenders' courage is steeled by the protection offered by their fortifications and trenches.

The Defender adds 1 to the Leadership characteristic of their units whilst they are within 6" of a Fortification from their army.

Deadly Defences

The fortifications on this world are all connected to a planetary defence auger that guides their automated fire.

The Defender can add 1 to hit rolls made for **BUILDINGS** in their army in the Shooting phase.

Captured Fortification

An undefended stronghold is an asset for the attackers to capture and turn upon the foe.

At the start of most Stronghold Assault missions, Fortifications are under the control of the Defender. However, the Attacker can capture any unoccupied **BUILDING** in their Movement phase if all the models in one of their **INFANTRY** units ends their move within 3" of that building. If they do so, the building immediately comes under their control and the unit must, if able to do so, embark inside to garrison it (note that they must still obey all the normal restrictions listed on that building's datasheet). Buildings can potentially exchange hands several times over the course of the battle. Note that only buildings with the **TRANSPORT** keyword can be captured in this manner – other Fortifications are fully automated or have no interior to capture and garrison.

WARLORD TRAITS AND DETACHMENTS

If you are playing a Stronghold Assault mission, you can use the following Warlord Traits and Detachments when choosing your army, depending on whether you are the Attacker or the Defender.

STRONGHOLD ASSAULT ATTACKER WARLORD TRAITS

D3	WARLORD TRAIT
1	**Siege Breaker** You can re-roll failed charge rolls for friendly units that are within 6" of your Warlord when they declare a charge against a **Building**.
2	**Fortress Destroyer** You can re-roll wound rolls of 1 for friendly units that are within 6" of your Warlord when they target a **Building**.
3	**Stronghold Assault Attacker** You have one bonus Command Point – this can only be spent on a Stronghold Assault Stratagem.

STRONGHOLD ASSAULT DEFENDER WARLORD TRAITS

D3	WARLORD TRAIT
1	**Counterfire Master** You can re-roll failed hit rolls for friendly units within 6" of your Warlord (this includes any **Building** they are embarked within, and any other units embarked within the same building).
2	**Fortress Commander** If your Warlord is embarked within a **Building**, roll a dice each time that building loses a wound; on a 6+, the building does not lose a wound.
3	**Stronghold Assault Defender** You have one bonus Command Point – this can only be spent on a Stronghold Assault Stratagem.

STRONGHOLD ASSAULT ATTACKER DETACHMENT

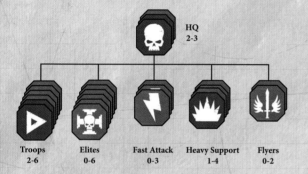

HQ
2-3

Troops 2-6   Elites 0-6   Fast Attack 0-3   Heavy Support 1-4   Flyers 0-2

Dedicated Transports: May include 1 for each other choice.

Restrictions: All units must be from the same Faction.

Command Benefits: +5 Command Points (these 5 CPs can only be spent on Stronghold Assault Stratagems).

STRONGHOLD ASSAULT DEFENDER DETACHMENT

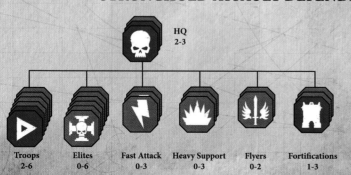

HQ
2-3

Troops 2-6   Elites 0-6   Fast Attack 0-3   Heavy Support 0-3   Flyers 0-2   Fortifications 1-3

Dedicated Transports: May include 1 for each other choice.

Restrictions: All units must be from the same Faction (excluding **Unaligned** units).

Command Benefits: +5 Command Points (these 5 CPs can only be spent on Stronghold Assault Stratagems).

STRATAGEMS

If you are playing a Stronghold Assault mission, you can spend Command Points (CPs) to use the following Stratagems, depending on whether you are the Attacker or the Defender.

PRELIMINARY BOMBARDMENT
3CP

Stronghold Assault Attacker Stratagem

Use this Stratagem at the start of the first battle round, but before the first turn begins. You can launch a Preliminary Bombardment, as described in the Narrative Play Mission Rules section of the *Warhammer 40,000* rulebook.

GREMLIN CURSE
1CP

Stronghold Assault Attacker Stratagem

Use this Stratagem at the start of any phase. Select a BUILDING; until the end of the current phase that building will only hit on rolls of 6, regardless of any modifier.

DESPERATE LAST PUSH
2CP

Stronghold Assault Attacker Stratagem

This Stratagem can only be used once per battle, and can only be used if the mission instructs either player to roll a D6 to determine if another battle round is played or if the battle ends. That player does not roll a dice – you automatically play another battle round.

DAWN ASSAULT
2CP

Stronghold Assault Attacker Stratagem

Use this Stratagem at the start of the first battle round, but before the first turn begins. For the duration of the first battle round, both players must use the Low Visibility rules from Battlezone: Night Fight, as described in the Battlezone section of the *Warhammer 40,000* rulebook.

STRUCTURAL COLLAPSE
1CP

Stronghold Assault Attacker Stratagem

Use this Stratagem when an attack causes a BUILDING to lose a wound. Roll 2D6; if the result is greater than that building's remaining wounds its Toughness characteristic is reduced by D3.

SAPPERS
2CP

Stronghold Assault Attacker Stratagem

Use this Stratagem before one of your units fights in the Fight phase. You can add 1 to wound rolls for that unit when it attacks a BUILDING that phase.

CONCEALED DEPLOYMENT
3CP

Stronghold Assault Defender Stratagem

Use this Stratagem after setting up all your Fortifications, but before deploying any other unit. Use the Concealed Deployment rules, as described in the Narrative Play Mission Rules section of the *Warhammer 40,000* rulebook, to deploy the rest of your units. If you want a unit to start the battle embarked inside a BUILDING, place its set-up marker on that building.

RIGGED TO BLOW
1CP

Stronghold Assault Defender Stratagem

Use this Stratagem when an enemy unit captures one of your BUILDINGS and embarks within it. Roll a D6; on a 1 nothing happens, otherwise the embarked unit suffers D6 mortal wounds.

FORTIFIED STRONGHOLD
2CP

Stronghold Assault Defender Stratagem

Use this Stratagem after you have set up a BUILDING. Whoever controls that building can add 1 to saving throws made for it for the duration of the battle.

AMMO STORE
2CP

Stronghold Assault Defender Stratagem

Use this Stratagem when a unit from your army that is embarked within a BUILDING shoots. You can re-roll failed hit rolls for that unit until the end of the phase.

EMERGENCY REPAIRS
1CP

Stronghold Assault Defender Stratagem

Use this Stratagem at the start of any of your turns. Select a BUILDING that has at least one unit from your army embarked in it; that building repairs one lost wound.

ESCAPE HATCH
3CP

Stronghold Assault Defender Stratagem

Use this Stratagem when one of your BUILDINGS is destroyed. Do not roll any dice for disembarking units to see if they are slain – all models automatically disembark safely.

STRONGHOLD ASSAULT
BREAKTHROUGH

The initial phase of the war has gone well, but now the attackers must cross no-man's-land quickly, under heavy fire, to break through the defenders' front lines.

THE ARMIES

The players choose armies as described on page 45.

THE BATTLEFIELD

The Defender creates the battlefield. They start by setting up their Fortifications anywhere on the battlefield wholly within their own table half. They then set up other terrain on the battlefield – we suggest plenty of barricades and obstacles, and a few ruins or craters. Next, the Defender places three objective markers. One may be placed in each **Building**. Any remaining objective markers are placed in the Defender's deployment zone; the centre of each must be more than 6" from the centre of any other objective marker, any building or any battlefield edge. If a building containing an objective marker is destroyed during the battle, the Defender must place the objective marker where the building used to be.

DEPLOYMENT

After the battlefield has been created, the Defender sets up their army wholly within their deployment zone. The Attacker then sets up their army wholly within their deployment zone.

FIRST TURN

The Defender has the first turn.

PUNCH THROUGH THEIR DEFENCES

The Attacker's units can move off the Defender's battlefield edge if all of their models can make it off the board in the same phase. Any that do so are removed from the board and take no further part in the battle.

GROUND TO COVER

If any of the Attacker's units have an ability that would enable them to move on from a battlefield edge, that unit can only move on from the Attacker's edge.

BATTLE LENGTH

The game lasts for six battle rounds.

VICTORY CONDITIONS

At the end of the game, the player who has scored the most victory points is the winner. If both players have the same number of victory points, the game is a draw. Victory points are achieved for the following:

Hold the Line: At the end of the game, the Defender scores 3 victory points for each objective marker they control. The Defender controls an objective marker if they have more models within 3" of the centre of it than the Attacker does. If an objective marker is within a **Building**, count all the models within 3" of it and all the models garrisoning it.

Break Through: At the end of the game, the Attacker scores 1 victory point for each of their units that is wholly within the Defender's deployment zone, and D3 victory points for each of their units that have moved off the Defender's battlefield edge (see above).

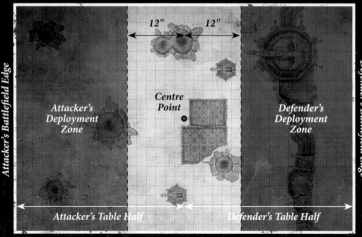

STRONGHOLD ASSAULT
BUNKER ASSAULT

One side has withdrawn behind the shelter of unyielding bunkers, holding the advancing foe at arm's reach whilst calling down withering salvoes of artillery strikes. The attackers must destroy or overwhelm the bunkers as quickly as possible, before the barrages pound them into oblivion.

THE ARMIES

The players choose armies as described on page 45.

THE BATTLEFIELD

The Defender creates the battlefield. They start by setting up their Fortifications anywhere on the battlefield wholly within their own table half. They then set up other terrain on the battlefield – we suggest plenty of barricades and obstacles, and a few ruins or craters.

DEPLOYMENT

After the battlefield has been created, the Defender sets up their army wholly within their deployment zone. The Attacker then sets up their army wholly within their deployment zone.

TARGETING AUGER

After both sides have deployed, the Defender selects one of their **Buildings** to house the Targeting Auger. Whilst this Fortification is garrisoned by one of the Defender's units, they can direct an artillery strike at the start of each of their Shooting phases in addition to any shooting attacks they make this phase. The Defender places a marker (such as a dice or coin) anywhere on the battlefield. The Attacker can move the marker D6" in any direction. After this is done, the Defender rolls a dice for each unit within 3" of the marker – on a 3+, that unit suffers D3 mortal wounds.

FIRST TURN

The Defender rolls a D6. On a 1, 2 or 3, the Attacker has the first turn, and on a 4, 5 or 6 the Defender has the first turn.

BATTLE LENGTH

The game lasts for six battle rounds.

VICTORY CONDITIONS

At the end of the game, the player who has scored the most victory points is the winner. If both players have the same number of victory points, the game is a draw. Victory points are achieved for the following:

No Quarter Given: Each player scores 1 victory point for each enemy unit that is destroyed.

Rubble and Ruin: The Attacker scores 3 victory points for each **Building** they destroy, and for each building they have captured and still hold at the end of the game. The Defender scores 3 victory points for each **Building** still on the battlefield at the end of the game not captured by the Attacker. Any **Building** with a Wounds characteristic of more than 15 is instead worth 6 victory points in each case.

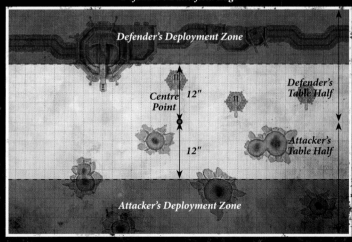

Defender's Battlefield Edge

Defender's Deployment Zone

Centre Point

12"

Defender's Table Half

12"

Attacker's Table Half

Attacker's Deployment Zone

Attacker's Battlefield Edge

ALL-OUT ATTACK

The defenders have withdrawn to a more heavily fortified position. For the attacking forces to push further, these strongholds must be overcome, despite the heavy losses that a headlong assault may incur.

THE ARMIES

The players choose armies as described on page 45.

THE BATTLEFIELD

The Defender creates the battlefield. They start by setting up their Fortifications anywhere on the battlefield wholly within their own table half. They then set up other terrain on the battlefield – we suggest plenty of barricades and obstacles, and a few ruins or craters. Next, the Defender places three objective markers. One may be placed in each **BUILDING**. Any remaining objective markers are placed in the Defender's deployment zone; the centre of each must be more than 6" from the centre of any other objective marker, any building or any battlefield edge. If a building containing an objective marker is destroyed during the battle, the Defender must place the objective marker where the building use to be.

DEPLOYMENT

After the battlefield has been created, the Defender sets up their army wholly within their deployment zone. The Attacker then sets up their army wholly within their deployment zone.

FIRST TURN

The Attacker has the first turn.

SUSTAINED ASSAULT

Any of the Attacker's units that are destroyed can later return to the battle. At the end of each of their Movement phases, the Attacker rolls a dice for each of their destroyed units, adding 2 to the result if that unit has the Troops Battlefield Role. On a 5+, they can immediately set that unit up again, wholly within 6" of their battlefield edge.

The Attacker can, at the end of any of their turns, remove any of their units from the battlefield that have a quarter or less of their starting number of models (or, in the case of single-model units, a quarter or less of its starting number of wounds). This unit then counts as having been destroyed for all purposes, and can be returned to the battle later as described above.

BATTLE LENGTH

The Attacker rolls a D6 at the end of battle round 5; on a 3+, the game continues, otherwise the game ends. At the end of battle round 6, the Defender rolls a D6; this time the game continues on a 4+, otherwise it ends. The battle automatically ends at the end of battle round 7.

VICTORY CONDITIONS

At the end of the game, the player who controls the most objective markers is the winner. If both players control the same number, the game is a draw. A player controls an objective marker if they have more models within 3" of the centre of it than their opponent does. If an objective marker is within a **BUILDING**, count all the models within 3" of it and all the models garrisoning it.

Defender's Battlefield Edge

Defender's Deployment Zone

Defender's Table Half

Centre Point 12"

30"

6"

Attacker's Table Half

Attacker's Deployment Zone

Attacker's Battlefield Edge

STRONGHOLD ASSAULT
CROSSFIRE

Networks of interconnected fortifications guard a vital crossing– a narrow pass with overlapping fields of fire. In preparation for a major push, the attacker must breach this cordon without suffering heavy casualties, overwhelming each fortified 'island' in turn while avoiding being caught in lethal crossfire.

THE ARMIES

The players choose armies as described on page 45.

THE BATTLEFIELD

The Defender creates the battlefield. They start by setting up their Fortifications anywhere on the battlefield wholly within their own table half or deployment zones. They then set up other terrain on the battlefield – we suggest plenty of barricades and obstacles, and a few ruins or craters.

DEPLOYMENT

After the battlefield has been created, the Defender sets up their army wholly within their three deployment zones (each 24" in diameter). At least one unit must be set up within each zone. The Attacker then sets up their army wholly within their deployment zone.

FORCED MARCH

Each time one of their units Advances, the Attacker rolls 2D6 and adds the scores together when determining how much further the unit can move.

FIRST TURN

The Attacker has the first turn.

GROUND TO COVER

If any of the Attacker's units have an ability that would enable them to move on from a battlefield edge, that unit can only move on from the Attacker's edge.

PUNCH THROUGH THEIR DEFENCES

The Attacker's units can move off the Defender's battlefield edge if all of their models can make it off the board in the same phase. Any that do so are removed from the board and take no further part in the battle.

BATTLE LENGTH

The game lasts for eight battle rounds.

VICTORY CONDITIONS

At the end of the game, the player who has scored the most victory points is the winner. If both players have the same number of victory points, the game is a draw. Victory points are achieved for the following:

Secure the Pass: At the end of the game, the Attacker scores 3 victory points for each of the Defender's deployment zones that contain no units from the Defender's army. The Defender scores 3 victory points for each one that does.

Killing Fields: The Defender scores 1 victory point for each enemy unit that is destroyed.

Break Through: At the end of the game, the Attacker scores 1 victory point for each of their units that is wholly within the break-through zone shown on the map, and D3 victory points for each of their units that has moved off the Defender's battlefield edge (see above).

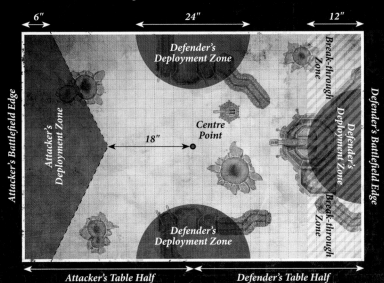

STRONGHOLD ASSAULT
THE BIG PUSH

After days of constant bombardment, the attackers have gathered their forces to launch an assault on the shattered remnants of the defending forces. Command has underestimated the tenacity of the foe, however, and as the attack begins the defenders are working to bring their weapons back online.

THE ARMIES

The players choose armies as described on page 45.

THE BATTLEFIELD

The Defender creates the battlefield. They start by setting up their Fortifications anywhere on the battlefield wholly within their own table half. They then set up other terrain on the battlefield – we suggest plenty of barricades and obstacles, and a few ruins or craters.

DEPLOYMENT

After the battlefield has been created, the Defender sets up their army wholly within their deployment zone. The Attacker then sets up their army wholly within their deployment zone.

SHATTERED DEFENCES

All of the Defender's BUILDINGS start the game dilapidated; their Toughness characteristic is reduced by 1 for the entire battle and they cannot fire any ranged weapons until the fourth battle round.

BUNKER BUSTER BOMBARDMENT

At the start of the first battle round, but before the first turn begins, the Attacker rolls a dice for each enemy BUILDING that is on the battlefield. On a roll of 4+, that building is hit by a bombardment; roll 2 dice and discard the lowest result – the building suffers that many mortal wounds.

FIRST TURN

The Defender rolls a D6. On a 1, 2 or 3, the Attacker has the first turn, and on a 4, 5 or 6 the Defender has the first turn.

BATTLE LENGTH

The Attacker rolls a D6 at the end of battle round 5; on a 3+, the game continues, otherwise the game ends. At the end of battle round 6, the Defender rolls a D6; this time the game continues on a 4+, otherwise it ends. The battle automatically ends at the end of battle round 7.

VICTORY CONDITIONS

At the end of the game, the player who has scored the most victory points is the winner. If both players have the same number of victory points, the game is a draw. Victory points are achieved for the following:

No Quarter Given: Each player scores 1 victory point for each enemy unit that is destroyed.

Battered but Defiant: At the end of the game the Defender scores 3 victory points for each BUILDING still on the battlefield that has not been captured.

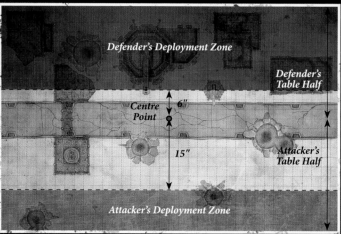

Defender's Battlefield Edge

Defender's Deployment Zone

Defender's Table Half

Centre Point

6"

15"

Attacker's Table Half

Attacker's Deployment Zone

Attacker's Battlefield Edge

STRONGHOLD ASSAULT
LAST STAND

Surrounded and besieged, a handful of troops have held out against all the odds. But now, the enemy have amassed in overwhelming numbers to stamp out this last vestige of resistance, and the defenders' reinforcements have been delayed. Until they arrive, the last survivors of the garrison are on their own.

THE ARMIES

The players choose armies as described on page 45. The Defender must include at least three INFANTRY units in their army.

THE BATTLEFIELD

The Defender creates the battlefield. They start by setting up their Fortifications anywhere on the battlefield wholly within their own table half. They then set up other terrain on the battlefield – we suggest plenty of barricades and obstacles, and a few ruins or craters.

DEPLOYMENT

After the battlefield has been created, the Defender sets up three INFANTRY units wholly within their deployment zone – these are the Last Survivors. The remainder of their army is placed in Reserve and will arrive as reinforcements, as described below. The Attacker then sets up their army wholly within their deployment zone.

FIRST TURN

The Defender has the first turn.

DELAYED RESERVES

At the end of each of their Movement phases, the Defender rolls a D6 for each of their Reserve units – this is called a Reserve roll. On a 3+, the unit being rolled for arrives from Reserve. Note that if a unit placed into Reserve is embarked within a TRANSPORT, they will arrive when their transport does, not separately (if rolling, make a single roll for the transport and the units embarked in it). Units arriving from Reserve are set up wholly within 6" of the Defender's battlefield edge.

LAST SURVIVORS

The Defender can re-roll failed Morale tests for their Last Survivor units.

BATTLE LENGTH

The Attacker rolls a D6 at the end of battle round 5; on a 2+, the game continues, otherwise the game ends. At the end of battle round 6, the Defender rolls a D6; this time the game continues on a 3+, otherwise it ends. The battle automatically ends at the end of battle round 7.

VICTORY CONDITIONS

At the end of the game, the Attacker wins if all three of the Last Survivor units have been completely destroyed. If two Last Survivor units have been completely destroyed the game is a draw, otherwise the Defender is the winner.

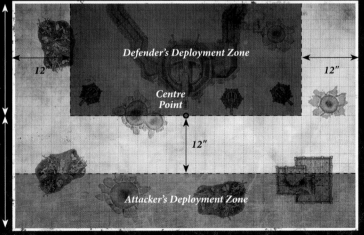

Defender's Battlefield Edge

Defender's Deployment Zone

12"

12"

Defender's Table Half

Centre Point

Attacker's Table Half

12"

Attacker's Deployment Zone

Attacker's Battlefield Edge

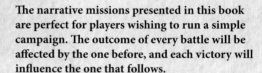

LINEAR CAMPAIGNS

PLANETSTRIKE: PLANETFALL

Attacker Victory: In Desperate Assault, the Attacker doubles the bonus Command Points they get from the Wrack and Ruin ability.

Defender Victory: In Desperate Assault, the Wrack and Ruin ability is not used.

PLANETSTRIKE: DESPERATE ASSAULT

Attacker Victory: In Seize and Destroy, the Attacker can re-roll any failed Reserve roll.

Defender Victory: In Seize and Destroy, the Defender adds 1 to the Toughness characteristic of the Vital Stronghold, if it is a **BUILDING**.

PLANETSTRIKE: SEIZE AND DESTROY

Attacker Victory: In Stranglehold, the Backs to the Walls ability is not used.

Defender Victory: In Stranglehold, the Attacker cannot use the Demolition Crew Stratagem.

PLANETSTRIKE: STRANGLEHOLD

Attacker Victory: In Forlorn Hope, when a model from the Attacker's army is the banner bearer, they can add 1 to saving throws made for that model's unit.

Defender Victory: In Forlorn Hope, the Defender can re-roll hit rolls of 1 and wound rolls of 1 when targeting the banner bearer, or their unit, with shooting and/or close combat attacks.

PLANETSTRIKE: FORLORN HOPE

Attacker Victory: In Planetquake, the Attacker has two bonus Command Points. In addition, the Attacker starts rolling for Tectonic Upheaval at the start of their second turn, instead of their third.

Defender Victory: In Planetquake, the Defender has two bonus Command Points. In addition, the Attacker must subtract 1 from any roll they make on the Tectonic Upheaval table (to a minimum of 1).

The narrative missions presented in this book are perfect for players wishing to run a simple campaign. The outcome of every battle will be affected by the one before, and each victory will influence the one that follows.

The Planetstrike and Stronghold Assault missions in this book can be played sequentially to tell a thrilling linear campaign. This is an extremely simple campaign where one player takes the role of Attacker in every mission and their opponent the Defender. The victor of the first battle will gain an advantage in the second battle in the campaign, making it easier to secure another victory and so gain another winner's bonus for the next battle, and so on. The campaign then culminates in a winner-takes-all final fight.

Planetstrike Campaign

To play a linear Planetstrike Campaign, first decide who will be the Attacker and who will be the Defender. Players cannot switch roles during the campaign.

Each player should then select one **CHARACTER** model in their collection to be their Supreme Warlord. Your Supreme Warlord has been chosen for their skill at global conquest or defence. As a result, at the beginning of the campaign they will have not one, but two Warlord Traits. One of these will be chosen from the Planetstrike Attacker or Defender table, as appropriate, and the other can be chosen from a different Warlord Traits table. Your Supreme Warlord has both of these traits throughout the campaign. If your Supreme Warlord is removed as a casualty during any of your games, roll a D6 at the end of the battle. On a 2+, the Supreme Warlord is assumed to have made a full recovery in time for the next battle in the campaign. On a 1, however, their injuries are more serious and will take more time to heal – your Supreme Warlord cannot be used in the next mission in the campaign and you will need to use a different model as your Warlord – generate a new Warlord Trait for them as normal.

Then simply play each of the Planetstrike missions in order. The victor of each mission earns a bonus in the next mission of the campaign, as detailed on the left. If a game is a draw, both players receive their bonus for the next mission. Whoever wins the final mission, Planetquake, is then the victor of the campaign. If this game ends in a draw, we suggest that whoever won the most victories during the previous missions is crowned overall victor. If this is still a draw, we suggest the Defender wins a moral victory – after all, their forces have likely been outnumbered throughout the campaign.

Stronghold Assault Campaign

To play a linear Stronghold Assault Campaign, simply follow the process detailed for a Planetstrike Campaign, except that in this campaign the Supreme Warlord takes one of their two Warlord Traits from the appropriate Stronghold Assault Attacker or Defender table. Play each of the Stronghold Assault missions in order, gaining the bonuses as detailed on the right. Whoever wins the final mission, Last Stand, is the winner of the campaign (in the case of a draw, use the process described on the left to determine the victor).

Planetary Invasion Campaign

If you're feeling adventurous, you can play both of these campaigns one after the other in a truly legendary Planetary Invasion campaign. In such a contest, the Planetstrike campaign is but the first phase of the war, where the invader lands their forces on the planet while the defender tries to repel them. The final phase of the war is the Stronghold Assault campaign, where the Attacker must consolidate their forces and attempt to break past the Defender's fortifications to crush them.

If you are playing a Planetary Invasion campaign, then players should retain their roles, Attacker or Defender, for both phases of the campaign. Each Supreme Warlord should have three Warlord Traits rather than two; one from the Planetstrike Attacker or Defender table, one from the Stronghold Assault Attacker or Defender table, and one from another Warlord Traits table. Whoever wins the Planetstrike phase wins one Laurel of Victory, and the appropriate bonus:

Attacker Bonus: In Breakthrough, the Attacker can make three Firestorm attacks, even though it is not a Planetstrike Mission. These attacks should be made after the Defender has deployed. In addition, the Attacker rolls a D6 at the end of each battle they lose during the Stronghold Assault phase. On a 5+ they get the bonus for the next game, even though they lost the last one.

Defender Bonus: In Breakthrough, the Defender selects a single **BUILDING** in their army. They can add 1 to save rolls for that building during the battle. In addition, the Defender rolls a D6 at the end of each battle they lose during the Stronghold Assault phase. On a 5+ they get the bonus for the next game, even though they lost the last one.

Whoever wins the Stronghold Assault phase of the campaign wins one Laurel of Victory. The player with the most Laurels of Victory at the end of both phases is the winner. If this is a tie, we suggest that whoever won the most victories throughout the entire campaign wins; if this is still a tie, the Defender earns a moral victory.

STRONGHOLD ASSAULT: BREAKTHROUGH

Attacker Victory: In Bunker Assault, the Attacker can move the Targeting Auger marker 2D6", instead of D6", as described in the Targeting Auger ability.

Defender Victory: In Bunker Assault, the Attacker can move the Targeting Auger marker D3", instead of D6", as described in the Targeting Auger Ability.

STRONGHOLD ASSAULT: BUNKER ASSAULT

Attacker Victory: In All-out Attack, the Attacker needs to roll a 4+ rather than a 5+ to return their destroyed units to battle as described in the Sustained Assault ability.

Defender Victory: In All-out Attack, the Attacker needs to roll a 6+ rather than a 5+ to return their destroyed units to battle as described in the Sustained Assault ability.

STRONGHOLD ASSAULT: ALL-OUT ATTACK

Attacker Victory: In Crossfire, the game lasts for nine battle rounds instead of eight. In addition, the Attacker rolls three dice rather than two each time one of their units Advances. They must discard the lowest result, then add the other two dice together when determining how much further the unit can move.

Defender Victory: In Crossfire, the game lasts for seven battle rounds instead of eight. In addition, the Forced March ability is not used.

STRONGHOLD ASSAULT: CROSSFIRE

Attacker Victory: In The Big Push, the Attacker's Bunker Buster Bombardment hits enemy **BUILDINGS** on the roll of a 2+, instead of a 4+.

Defender Victory: In The Big Push, the Shattered Defences ability is not used.

STRONGHOLD ASSAULT: THE BIG PUSH

Attacker Victory: In The Last Stand, the Attacker has two bonus Command Points. In addition, the Defender must subtract 1 from all their Reserve rolls.

Defender Victory: In The Last Stand, the Defender has two bonus Command Points. In addition, the Defender adds 1 to all their Reserve rolls.

AEGIS DEFENCE LINE

4 POWER

NAME	M	WS	BS	S	T	W	A	Ld	Sv
Gun Emplacement	-	-	5+	-	7	3	-	-	4+

An Aegis Defence Line consists of 4 large shield sections and 4 small shield sections. It may also include one gun emplacement. All shield sections of an Aegis Defence Line must be set up so that they are in end-to-end contact with at least one other shield section, while the gun emplacement must be set up within 6" of any shield section. The gun emplacement is equipped with an Icarus lascannon.

WEAPON	RANGE	TYPE	S	AP	D	ABILITIES
Icarus lascannon	96"	Heavy 1	9	-3	D6	Add 1 to hit rolls made for this weapon against targets that can **FLY**. Subtract 1 from hit rolls made for this weapon against all other targets.
Quad-gun	48"	Heavy 8	7	-1	1	Add 1 to hit rolls made for this weapon against targets that can **FLY**. Subtract 1 from hit rolls made for this weapon against all other targets.

WARGEAR OPTIONS	• The gun emplacement may replace its Icarus lascannon with a quad-gun.

ABILITIES	**Static Defence Network:** After it is set up, an Aegis Defence Line (excluding its gun emplacement, if any) is treated as a terrain feature. It cannot move for any reason, is not treated as a friendly or enemy model, and cannot be targeted or affected by any attacks or abilities. **Immobile:** This model cannot move for any reason, nor can it fight in the Fight phase. Enemy models automatically hit this model in the Fight phase – do not make hit rolls. However, this model can still shoot if there are enemy models within 1" of it, and friendly units can still target enemy units that are within 1" of this model.	**Automated Weapons:** Unless a friendly **INFANTRY** model is within 1" of a gun emplacement, it can only target the nearest visible enemy unit. If two units are equally close, you may chose which is targeted. **Defence Line:** **INFANTRY** units within 1" of an Aegis Defence Line, and behind it from the point of view of the firing unit, receive the benefit of cover. When charging a unit on the opposite side of an Aegis Defence Line, the charge is successful if the charging unit can move within 2" of that unit. When resolving fights between units on opposite sides of an Aegis Defence Line, units can be chosen to fight and make their attacks if the enemy is within 2" instead of the normal 1".

FACTION KEYWORDS	**UNALIGNED**
KEYWORDS (DEFENCE LINE)	**AEGIS DEFENCE LINE**
KEYWORDS (GUN EMPLACEMENT)	**VEHICLE, GUN EMPLACEMENT**

An Imperial regiment prepares to fend off a planetary invasion, presenting a bristling wall of lasguns and artillery to the foe.

IMPERIAL BASTION

10 POWER

NAME	M	WS	BS	S	T	W	A	Ld	Sv
Imperial Bastion	-	-	5+	-	9	20	-	-	3+

An Imperial Bastion is a single model equipped with four heavy bolters.

WEAPON	RANGE	TYPE	S	AP	D	ABILITIES
Heavy bolter	36"	Heavy 3	5	-1	1	-
Icarus lascannon	96"	Heavy 1	9	-3	D6	Add 1 to hit rolls made for this weapon against targets that can **FLY**. Subtract 1 from hit rolls made for this weapon against all other targets.
Quad-gun	48"	Heavy 8	7	-1	1	Add 1 to hit rolls made for this weapon against targets that can **FLY**. Subtract 1 from hit rolls made for this weapon against all other targets.

WARGEAR OPTIONS	• This model may take an Icarus lascannon or a quad-gun.
ABILITIES	**Immobile:** This model cannot move for any reason, nor can it fight in the Fight phase. Enemy models automatically hit this model in the Fight phase – do not make hit rolls. However, this model can still shoot if there are enemy models within 1" of it, and friendly units can still target enemy units that are within 1" of this model. **Automated Weapons:** Unless a friendly unit is embarked inside this model, each of its weapons can only target the nearest visible enemy. If two units are equally close, you may choose which is targeted. **Fire Points:** 10 models embarked in this model can shoot in their Shooting phase, measuring range and drawing line of sight from any point on this model. They can do this even if enemy models are within 1" of this model. **Magazine Explosion:** If this model is reduced to 0 wounds, roll a D6 before removing it from the battlefield and before any embarked models disembark. On a 6 its magazine explodes, and each unit within 2D6" suffers D3 mortal wounds. **Designer's Note:** *If you cannot physically remove this model from your battlefield when it is destroyed (because, for example, it is glued to the surface) then regardless of whether its magazine explodes or not, it is wrecked – from that point on, models can no longer embark inside it, it can no longer shoot etc.*
TRANSPORT	This model can transport any number of **INFANTRY CHARACTERS** and one other **INFANTRY** unit, up to a maximum of 20 models. **Designer's Note:** *When you embark models onto an Imperial Bastion, you may find it useful to place some of them on the battlements to remind you which unit(s) are inside the fortification.*
FACTION KEYWORDS	**UNALIGNED**
KEYWORDS	**BUILDING, VEHICLE, TRANSPORT, IMPERIAL BASTION**

IMPERIAL DEFENCE LINE

4 POWER

An Imperial Defence Line consists of 2 trench sections and up to 4 end sections, or 3 defence emplacement sections and up to 2 additional end sections. All sections must be set up so that they are in end-to-end contact with at least one other **WALL OF MARTYRS** model.

ABILITIES	**Static Defence Network:** After it is set up, an Imperial Defence Line is treated as a terrain feature. It cannot move for any reason, is not treated as a friendly or enemy model, and cannot be targeted or affected by any attacks or abilities. **Stalwart Defence:** **IMPERIUM INFANTRY** units add 1 to their Leadership whilst they are within an Imperial Defence Line.	**Defence Line:** **INFANTRY** units within an Imperial Defence Line, and behind it from the point of view of the firing unit, receive the benefit of cover. When charging a unit within an Imperial Defence Line, the charge is successful if the charging unit can move within 2" of that unit. When resolving fights between units on opposite sides of an Imperial Defence Line, units can be chosen to fight and make their attacks if the enemy is within 2" instead of the normal 1".
FACTION KEYWORDS	**UNALIGNED**	
KEYWORDS	**WALL OF MARTYRS, IMPERIAL DEFENCE LINE**	

IMPERIAL BUNKER

5 POWER

NAME	M	WS	BS	S	T	W	A	Ld	Sv
Imperial Bunker	-		5+	-	8	12	-	-	3+

An Imperial Bunker is a single model.

WEAPON	RANGE	TYPE	S	AP	D	ABILITIES
Icarus lascannon	96"	Heavy 1	9	-3	D6	Add 1 to hit rolls made for this weapon against targets that can **FLY**. Subtract 1 from hit rolls made for this weapon against all other targets.
Quad-gun	48"	Heavy 8	7	-1	1	Add 1 to hit rolls made for this weapon against targets that can **FLY**. Subtract 1 from hit rolls made for this weapon against all other targets.

WARGEAR OPTIONS	• This model may take an Icarus lascannon or a quad-gun.

ABILITIES	**Immobile:** This model cannot move for any reason, nor can it fight in the Fight phase. Enemy models automatically hit this model in the Fight phase – do not make hit rolls. However, this model can still shoot if there are enemy models within 1" of it, and friendly units can still target enemy units that are within 1" of this model. *Designer's Note: If you cannot physically remove this model from your battlefield when it is destroyed (because, for example, it is glued to the surface) then regardless of whether it explodes or not, it is wrecked – from that point on, models can no longer embark inside it, it can no longer shoot etc.*	**Fire Points:** 5 models embarked in this model can shoot in their Shooting phase, measuring range and drawing line of sight from any point on this model. They can do this even if enemy models are within 1" of this model. **Explodes:** If this model is reduced to 0 wounds, roll a D6 before removing it from the battlefield and before any embarked models disembark. On a 6 it explodes, and each unit within D6" suffers D3 mortal wounds. **Automated Weapons:** Unless a friendly unit is embarked inside this model, each of its weapons can only target the nearest visible enemy. If two units are equally close, you may choose which is targeted. *Designer's Note: When you embark models onto an Imperial Bunker, you may find it useful to place some of them on the battlements to remind you which unit(s) are inside the fortification.*
TRANSPORT	This model can transport any number of **INFANTRY CHARACTERS** and one other **INFANTRY** unit, up to a maximum of 10 models.	

FACTION KEYWORDS	**UNALIGNED**
KEYWORDS	**BUILDING, VEHICLE, TRANSPORT, WALL OF MARTYRS, IMPERIAL BUNKER**

VENGEANCE WEAPON BATTERIES

6 POWER

NAME	M	WS	BS	S	T	W	A	Ld	Sv
Vengeance Weapon Battery	-	-	5+	-	8	10	-	-	3+

A Vengeance Weapon Battery is a single model equipped with a punisher gatling cannon. It can include 1 additional Vengeance Weapon Battery (Power Rating +6).

WEAPON	RANGE	TYPE	S	AP	D	ABILITIES
Battle cannon	72"	Heavy D6	8	-2	D3	-
Punisher gatling cannon	24"	Heavy 20	5	0	1	-
Quad Icarus lascannon	96"	Heavy 4	9	-3	D6	Add 1 to all hit rolls made for this weapon against targets that can **FLY**. Subtract 1 from the hit rolls made for this weapon against all other targets.

WARGEAR OPTIONS	• This model may replace its punisher gatling cannon with a battle cannon or a quad Icarus lascannon.

ABILITIES	**Immobile:** This model cannot move for any reason, nor can it fight in the Fight phase. Enemy models automatically hit this model in the Fight phase – do not make hit rolls. However, this model can still shoot if there are enemy models within 1" of it, and friendly units can still target enemy units that are within 1" of this model. **Fully Automated Weapons:** This model's weapons can only target the nearest visible enemy. Quad Icarus lascannons can instead choose to target the nearest visible enemy that can **FLY**. In either case, if two units are equally close, you may choose which is targeted.	**Magazine Explosion:** If this model is reduced to 0 wounds, roll a D6 before removing it from the battlefield. On a 6 its magazine explodes, and each unit within 2D6" suffers D3 mortal wounds. **Designer's Note:** *If you cannot physically remove this model from your battlefield when it is destroyed (because, for example, it is glued to the surface) then regardless of whether its magazine explodes or not, it is wrecked – from that point on, models can no longer target it, it can no longer shoot etc.*

FACTION KEYWORDS	**UNALIGNED**
KEYWORDS	**BUILDING, VEHICLE, WALL OF MARTYRS, VENGEANCE WEAPON BATTERIES**

PLASMA OBLITERATOR

9 POWER

NAME	M	WS	BS	S	T	W	A	Ld	Sv
Plasma Obliterator	-	-	5+	-	9	20	-	-	3+

A Plasma Obliterator is a single model equipped with a plasma obliterator.

WEAPON	RANGE	TYPE	S	AP	D	ABILITIES
Plasma obliterator	72"	Heavy 2D6	8	-3	2	Each time you roll a hit roll of 1 when firing this weapon, this model suffers a mortal wound after all of its shots have been resolved.

ABILITIES	**Immobile:** This model cannot move for any reason, nor can it fight in the Fight phase. Enemy models automatically hit this model in the Fight phase – do not make hit rolls. However, this model can still shoot if there are enemy models within 1" of it, and friendly units can still target enemy units that are within 1" of this model. **Automated Weapons:** Unless a friendly unit is embarked inside this model, its weapon can only target the nearest visible enemy. If two units are equally close, you may choose which is targeted.	**Fire Points:** 10 models embarked in this model can shoot in their Shooting phase, measuring range and drawing line of sight from any point on this model. They can do this even if enemy models are within 1" of this model. **Plasma Explosion:** If this model is reduced to 0 wounds, roll a D6 before removing it from the battlefield and before any embarked models disembark. On a 4+ its plasma core explodes, and each unit within D6" suffers D6 mortal wounds.

TRANSPORT	This model can transport any number of **INFANTRY CHARACTERS** and one other **INFANTRY** unit, up to a maximum of 20 models.
FACTION KEYWORDS	**UNALIGNED**
KEYWORDS	**BUILDING, VEHICLE, TRANSPORT, PLASMA OBLITERATOR**

FIRESTORM REDOUBT

15 POWER

NAME	M	WS	BS	S	T	W	A	Ld	Sv
Firestorm Redoubt	-	-	5+	-	8	20	-	-	3+

A Firestorm Redoubt is a single model equipped with two quad Icarus lascannons.

WEAPON	RANGE	TYPE	S	AP	D	ABILITIES
Battle cannon	72"	Heavy D6	8	-2	D3	-
Punisher gatling cannon	24"	Heavy 20	5	0	1	-
Quad Icarus lascannon	96"	Heavy 4	9	-3	D6	Add 1 to all hit rolls made for this weapon against targets that can **FLY**. Subtract 1 from the hit rolls made for this weapon against all other targets.

WARGEAR OPTIONS	• This model may replace each quad Icarus lascannon with a battle cannon or a punisher gatling cannon.

ABILITIES	**Automated Weapons:** Unless a friendly unit is embarked inside this model, this model's weapons can only target the nearest visible enemy. Quad Icarus lascannons can instead choose to target the nearest visible enemy that can **FLY**. In either case, if two units are equally close, you may choose which is targeted. **Magazine Explosion:** If this model is reduced to 0 wounds, roll a D6 before removing it from the battlefield and before any embarked models disembark. On a 6 its magazine explodes, and each unit within 2D6" suffers D3 mortal wounds. **Fire Points:** 10 models embarked in this model can shoot in their Shooting phase, measuring range and drawing line of sight from any point on this model. They can do this even if enemy models are within 1" of this model.	**Immobile:** This model cannot move for any reason, nor can it fight in the Fight phase. Enemy models automatically hit this model in the Fight phase – do not make hit rolls. However, this model can still shoot if there are enemy models within 1" of it, and friendly units can still target enemy units that are within 1" of this model. **Designer's Note:** *If you cannot physically remove this model from your battlefield when it is destroyed (because, for example, it is glued to the surface) then regardless of whether its magazine explodes or not, it is wrecked – from that point on, models can no longer embark inside it, it can no longer shoot etc.*

TRANSPORT	This model can transport any number of **INFANTRY CHARACTERS** and one other **INFANTRY** unit, up to a maximum of 20 models. **Designer's Note:** *When you embark models onto a Firestorm Redoubt, you may find it useful to place some of them on the battlements to remind you which unit(s) are inside the fortification.*
FACTION KEYWORDS	**UNALIGNED**
KEYWORDS	**BUILDING, VEHICLE, TRANSPORT, WALL OF MARTYRS, FIRESTORM REDOUBT**

A Firestorm Redoubt's lascannons spit a hail of superheated death into the sky, blasting enemy aircraft to lumps of blackened metal.

MACRO-CANNON
AQUILA STRONGPOINT

NAME	M	WS	BS	S	T	W	A	Ld	Sv
Macro-cannon Aquila Strongpoint	-	-	5+	-	10	30	-	-	3+

A Macro-cannon Aquila Strongpoint is a single model equipped with an Aquila macro-cannon.

WEAPON	RANGE	TYPE	S	AP	D	ABILITIES
Aquila macro-cannon	When attacking with this weapon, choose one of the profiles below.					
- Macro shell	72"	Heavy D6	14	-3	D6	Treat any Damage rolls of 1 or 2 made for this weapon as 3 instead.
- Quake shell	180"	Heavy 2D6	9	-2	D3	-
Heavy bolter	36"	Heavy 3	5	-1	1	-

WARGEAR OPTIONS	• This model may take up to four heavy bolters.

ABILITIES	**Immobile:** This model cannot move for any reason, nor can it fight in the Fight phase. Enemy models automatically hit this model in the Fight phase – do not make hit rolls. However, this model can still shoot if there are enemy models within 1" of it, and friendly units can still target enemy units that are within 1" of this model. **Designer's Note:** *If you cannot physically remove this model from your battlefield when it is destroyed (because, for example, it is glued to the surface) then regardless of whether its magazine explodes or not, it is wrecked – from that point on, models can no longer embark inside it, it can no longer shoot etc.*	**Fire Points:** 15 models embarked in this model can shoot in their Shooting phase, measuring range and drawing line of sight from any point on this model. They can do this even if enemy models are within 1" of this model. **Magazine Explosion:** If this model is reduced to 0 wounds, roll a D6 before removing it from the battlefield and before any embarked models disembark. On a 6 its magazine explodes, and each unit within 2D6" suffers D6 mortal wounds. **Automated Weapons:** Unless a friendly unit is embarked inside this model, each of its weapons can only target the nearest visible enemy. If two units are equally close, you may choose which is targeted.

TRANSPORT	This model can transport any number of **INFANTRY CHARACTERS** and one other **INFANTRY** unit, up to a maximum of 30 models. **Designer's Note:** *When you embark models onto a Macro-cannon Aquila Strongpoint, you may find it useful to place some of them on the battlements to remind you which unit(s) are inside the fortification.*

FACTION KEYWORDS	**UNALIGNED**

KEYWORDS	**BUILDING, VEHICLE, TRANSPORT, WALL OF MARTYRS, AQUILA STRONGPOINT, MACRO-CANNON**

An Aquila Strongpoint is designed to obliterate enemy super-heavy armour with its fearsome macro-cannon.

VORTEX MISSILE AQUILA STRONGPOINT

NAME	M	WS	BS	S	T	W	A	Ld	Sv
Vortex Missile Aquila Strongpoint	-	-	5+	-	10	30	-	-	3+

A Vortex Missile Aquila Strongpoint is a single model equipped with a vortex missile battery.

WEAPON	RANGE	TYPE	S	AP	D	ABILITIES
Heavy bolter	36"	Heavy 3	5	-1	1	-
Vortex missile battery	180"	Heavy D6	-	-	-	This weapon may target units that are not visible to the bearer, even when firing in accordance with the Automated Weapons ability. Each time you hit the target with this weapon it suffers D6 mortal wounds. If a model is wounded but not slain by the attack, roll another dice; on a 6, the model suffers a further D6 mortal wounds.

WARGEAR OPTIONS	• This model may take up to four heavy bolters.

ABILITIES	**Containment Failure:** If this model is reduced to 0 wounds, before removing it from the battlefield and before any embarked models disembark, its vortex missiles explode. Each unit within 2D6" suffers D6 mortal wounds. If a model is wounded but not slain in this manner, roll another dice; on a roll of a 6, the model is sucked into the swirling vortex and slain. **Designer's Note:** *If you cannot physically remove this model from your battlefield when it is destroyed (because, for example, it is glued to the surface) then it is wrecked – from that point on, models can no longer embark inside it, it can no longer shoot etc.* **Automated Weapons:** Unless a friendly unit is embarked inside this model, each of its weapons can only target the nearest visible enemy. If two units are equally close, you may choose which is targeted.	**Fire Points:** 15 models embarked in this model can shoot in their Shooting phase, measuring range and drawing line of sight from any point on this model. They can do this even if enemy models are within 1" of this model. **Immobile:** This model cannot move for any reason, nor can it fight in the Fight phase. Enemy models automatically hit this model in the Fight phase – do not make hit rolls. However, this model can still shoot if there are enemy models within 1" of it, and friendly units can still target enemy units that are within 1" of this model.
TRANSPORT	This model can transport any number of **INFANTRY CHARACTERS** and one other **INFANTRY** unit, up to a maximum of 30 models. **Designer's Note:** *When you embark models onto a Vortex Missile Aquila Strongpoint, you may find it useful to place some of them on the battlements to remind you which unit(s) are inside the fortification.*	
FACTION KEYWORDS	**UNALIGNED**	
KEYWORDS	**BUILDING, VEHICLE, TRANSPORT, WALL OF MARTYRS, AQUILA STRONGPOINT, VORTEX MISSILE**	

VOID SHIELD GENERATOR

NAME	M	WS	BS	S	T	W	A	Ld	Sv
Void Shield Generator	-	-	-	-	8	18	-	-	4+

A Void Shield Generator is a single model.

ABILITIES	**Immobile:** This model cannot move for any reason, nor can it fight in the Fight phase. Enemy models automatically hit this model in the Fight phase – do not make hit rolls. Friendly units can still target enemy units that are within 1" of this model.	**Projected Void Shields:** All units wholly within 6" of a Void Shield Generator receive a 5+ invulnerable save against any attacks made in the Shooting phase (unless the firing model is also within 6" of the Void Shield Generator).
FACTION KEYWORDS	**UNALIGNED**	
KEYWORDS	**BUILDING, VEHICLE, VOID SHIELD GENERATOR**	

SKYSHIELD LANDING PAD

NAME	M	WS	BS	S	T	W	A	Ld	Sv
Skyshield Landing Pad	-	-	-	-	8	20	-	-	4+

A Skyshield Landing Pad is a single model.

ABILITIES	
	Landing Pad Configuration: At the start of your turn, if there are no enemy models within 1" of the Skyshield Landing Pad, a friendly model within 1" of it can change the Skyshield Landing Pad's configuration to one of the following:
	• **Shielded:** All models (friend or foe) that are on top of the Skyshield Landing Pad in this configuration receive a 5+ invulnerable save against any attacks made in the Shooting phase (unless the firing model is also on top of the Skyshield Landing Pad). Note, however, that the Skyshield Landing Pad itself does not receive an invulnerable save in this manner.
	• **Unfurled:** Any friendly unit with the Flyer Battlefield Role that spends its entire turn on top of a Skyshield Landing Pad in this configuration regains D3 lost wounds at the end of the turn as a result of the landing pad's auto-repair systems.
	Immobile: This model cannot move for any reason, nor can it fight in the Fight phase. Enemy models automatically hit this model in the Fight phase – do not make hit rolls. Friendly units can still target enemy units that are within 1" of this model.
	Wrecked Landing Pad: If a Skyshield Landing Pad is destroyed, do not remove the model. Instead, all of its other abilities cease to apply, and it is treated as ruins (see the Battlefield Terrain section of the Warhammer 40,000 rulebook) for the rest of the battle.
FACTION KEYWORDS	UNALIGNED
KEYWORDS	BUILDING, VEHICLE, SKYSHIELD LANDING PAD

Tempestus warriors disembark onto a Skyshield Landing Pad, ready to unleash their weapons into the oncoming enemy.

MATCHED PLAY

'When you meet the foe upon
the field of battle, seek keenly
for every advantage. When
shells are flying and blades are
drawn, such faithful diligence
can be the difference between
victory in the Emperor's name,
or ignominious defeat.'

- Warmaster Slaydo,
saviour of the Sabbat Worlds

NEW BATTLEFRONTS

Pitting two Battle-forged armies against one another, matched play missions are as level a playing field as you can get in your Warhammer 40,000 games. Victory will go to the commander who has fortune, strategy and cunning on their side, and each new mission you play is an opportunity to master all three.

From capturing enemy-held objectives to seizing precious relics with a worth calculated in worlds, dominating the battlefield with heavy artillery to annihilating your foes wholesale, the matched play missions available in the *Warhammer 40,000* rulebook give players a wide range of strategic challenges. Whether your tastes run to the tightly controlled scenarios of Eternal War, or the rapidly shifting battlefield challenges of Maelstrom of War, there's plenty of material there to keep you gaming for days on end.

Every general or warlord worth their name relishes new strategic challenges, however. Tried and tested tactics must be revised, or whole new routes to victory found. Units or weapons that seemed, at first glance, to lack the utility you desired suddenly come into their own as their abilities on the tabletop are proved invaluable. Opponents who know each other's every ploy suddenly discover new tricks and traps to try out on one another. On the following pages you will find just such a range of exciting new opportunities to crush your foes.

Amongst the Eternal War missions on offer, you will find battles in which reserve forces roll in turn after turn to escalate the conflict to catastrophic levels. You will play games where the location of your goals is concealed until the last moment, forcing you and your opponent into a race to secure them, and others in which the acquisition of certain objectives can bestow upon a warlord unparalleled glory. Commanders will be assassinated and territory claimed, with each battle offering new nail-biting chances for victory or defeat.

The Maelstrom of War missions presented here are equally exciting, introducing new permutations of this system to bring fresh challenge to your games. From battles in which forces must act quickly to secure their objectives before the chance to succeed passes them forever, to scenarios in which leaders must make strategic gambles to win, or forces must engage in a desperate race against time to evade a horrible death, these thrilling and chaotic battles will test your skills as a tabletop commander to the absolute limits!

PLAYING NEW MISSIONS

This section includes twelve new matched play missions; six Eternal War missions, and six Maelstrom of War missions. You can agree with your opponent which set of matched play missions to use, or you can roll off, and whoever rolls highest can choose which set to use, be it one from this book or the *Warhammer 40,000* rulebook.

Having picked the set you wish to use, you can either select one of the six missions, or roll a dice to randomly select one using the appropriate table. The table for the matched play missions in this book is below.

D6	ETERNAL WAR MISSION	MAELSTROM OF WAR MISSION
1	Front-line Warfare	Kill Confirmed
2	Resupply Drop	Targets of Opportunity
3	Scorched Earth	Tactical Gambit
4	Dominate and Destroy	Race to Victory
5	Ascension	Sealed Orders
6	Roving Patrol	Recon

MATCHED PLAY MISSION RULES

In addition to Psychic Focus, Strategic Discipline and Tactical Reserves, the following special rules also apply to all matched play games.

Understrength Support

Understrength units can only be included in Auxiliary Support Detachments.

Targeting Characters

An enemy CHARACTER with less than 10 wounds can only be targeted if it is both visible to the firer and it is the closest enemy model to the firer. This means that if any other enemy model is closer, whether it is visible or not, then the enemy CHARACTER cannot be targeted.

Limits of Command

You cannot use the Command Re-roll Stratagem to affect Mission dice rolls. Mission dice rolls include any dice rolls that are made before the battle begins (such as those that determine who chooses deployment zones or who gets the first turn), those that must be made at the end of a battle round (such as rolls that determine if the battle ends) or any rolls that determine how many victory points are awarded to a player.

Boots on the Ground

When determining which player controls an objective marker, exclude all units that have the Flyer Battlefield Role – these units can never control objective markers.

FRONT-LINE WARFARE

Your forces have encountered the enemy along a contested border between your territory and theirs. It is imperative that you seize the disputed ground quickly, while preventing your foe from crossing the border into your own lands.

THE ARMIES

Each player selects a Battle-forged army to an agreed points limit.

THE BATTLEFIELD

Create the battlefield and set up terrain.

The players roll off and the winner determines which of the standard deployment maps is used in the battle (see the *Warhammer 40,000* rulebook) and picks one of the deployment zones for their army. Their opponent uses the other deployment zone.

The players then place four objective markers on the battlefield as follows. Starting with the player who won the earlier roll-off, the players alternate placing these objective markers until all four have been set up. The first objective marker set up by each player can be placed anywhere on the battlefield so long as the centre of the marker is at least 12" from the centre of the battlefield and both players' deployment zones. The second objective marker set up by each player must be placed in their own deployment zone. In both cases the centre of each objective marker must be more than 12" from the centre of any other objective marker and more than 6" from the edge of the battlefield.

DEPLOYMENT

The players alternate deploying their units, one at a time, starting with the player who placed the fourth objective marker. A player's models must be set up wholly within their deployment zone. Continue setting up units until both sides have set up their army.

FIRST TURN

The players roll off, and the player who finished setting up their army first adds 1 to their result. The winner can choose to take the first or second turn. If they take the first turn, their opponent can roll a D6; on a 6, they manage to seize the initiative, and they get the first turn instead!

BATTLE LENGTH

At the end of battle round 5, the player who had the first turn rolls a D6. On a 3+, the game continues, otherwise the game is over. At the end of battle round 6, the player who had the second turn rolls a D6. This time the game continues on a 4+, otherwise the game is over. The battle automatically ends at the end of battle round 7.

VICTORY CONDITIONS

At the end of the game, the player with the most victory points is the winner. If both players have the same, the game is a draw. Victory points are scored for the following:

Seize and Control: At the end of the game, each objective marker is worth a number of victory points to the player who controls it. A player controls an objective marker if they have more models within 3" of the centre of it than their opponent does. The number of victory points you receive for each objective marker you control depends on its location: the objective marker in your own deployment zone is worth 1 victory point, the objective marker in the enemy's deployment zone is worth 4 victory points, and the other two objective markers are each worth 2 victory points.

Slay the Warlord: If the enemy Warlord has been slain during the battle, you score 1 victory point.

First Blood: The first unit, of any kind, to be destroyed during the battle is worth 1 victory point to the opposing player at the end of the game. If two or more units from opposing forces are destroyed simultaneously, then both players get 1 victory point.

Linebreaker: If, at the end of the battle, you have at least one model within the enemy's deployment zone, you score 1 victory point.

+++

IT IS BETTER TO PLANT YOUR FLAG ATOP A HILL OF FALLEN HEROES, THAN KEEP IT FURLED AMIDST AN ARMY OF COWARDS.

+++

ETERNAL WAR
RESUPPLY DROP

Braving the flak batteries of the foe, your best pilots are inbound with supplies to drop to your beleaguered forces. You must race your enemy to the prize, driving them away from the drop coordinates and seizing the supplies as they land.

THE ARMIES

Each player selects a Battle-forged army to an agreed points limit.

THE BATTLEFIELD

Create the battlefield and set up terrain. Next, the players place six objective markers as follows. The players roll off and, starting with the winner, the players alternate placing these objective markers until all six have been set up. The objective markers can be placed anywhere on the battlefield, as long as the centre of each is more than 12" from the centre of any other objective marker and more than 6" from the edge of the battlefield.

DEPLOYMENT

The player who placed the sixth objective marker determines which of the standard deployment maps is used in the battle (see the *Warhammer 40,000* rulebook) and picks one of the deployment zones for their army. Their opponent uses the other deployment zone.

The players alternate deploying their units, one at a time, starting with the player who did not pick their deployment zone. A player's models must be set up wholly within their deployment zone. Continue setting up units until both sides have set up their army.

FIRST TURN

The players roll off, and the player who finished setting up their army first adds 1 to their result. The winner can choose to take the first or second turn. If they take the first turn, their opponent can roll a D6; on a 6, they manage to seize the initiative, and they get the first turn instead!

SUPPLIES INCOMING

At the start of the third battle round, the player who has the next turn selects three objective markers. These are the alpha objective markers. The remaining three are the beta objective markers. That player then randomly selects an alpha objective marker by rolling a D3 – the other two are removed

from the battlefield. This is a Mission roll (pg 67), so cannot be re-rolled by using the Command Re-roll Stratagem. At the start of their opponent's next turn, their opponent does likewise for the beta objective markers. After this is done, there should only be two objective markers remaining on the battlefield – these are the supplies both players must now control.

BATTLE LENGTH

At the end of battle round 5, the player who had the first turn rolls a D6. On a 3+, the game continues, otherwise the game is over. At the end of battle round 6, the player who had the second turn rolls a D6. This time the game continues on a 4+, otherwise the game is over. The battle automatically ends at the end of battle round 7.

VICTORY CONDITIONS

At the end of the game, the player with the most victory points is the winner. If both players have the same, the game is a draw. Victory points are scored for the following:

Secure Supplies: At the end of the game, each of the two objective markers left on the battlefield is worth 3 victory points to the player who controls it. A player controls an objective marker if they have more models within 3" of the centre of it than their opponent does.

Slay the Warlord: If the enemy Warlord has been slain during the battle, you score 1 victory point.

First Blood: The first unit, of any kind, to be destroyed during the battle is worth 1 victory point to the opposing player at the end of the game. If two or more units from opposing forces are destroyed simultaneously, then both players get 1 victory point.

Linebreaker: If, at the end of the battle, you have at least one model within the enemy's deployment zone, you score 1 victory point.

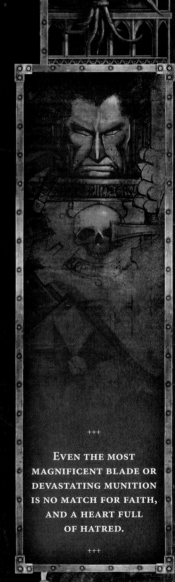

+++

EVEN THE MOST
MAGNIFICENT BLADE OR
DEVASTATING MUNITION
IS NO MATCH FOR FAITH,
AND A HEART FULL
OF HATRED.

+++

ETERNAL WAR
SCORCHED EARTH

You are fighting for control of key strategic assets scattered throughout this region. However, while seizing these locations is undoubtedly valuable, destroying those crucial to your enemy is more important still, and will likely bring you victory.

THE ARMIES

Each player selects a Battle-forged army to an agreed points limit.

THE BATTLEFIELD

Create the battlefield and set up terrain. Next, the players place six objective markers as follows. The players roll off and, starting with the winner, the players alternate placing these objective markers until all six have been set up. The objective markers can be placed anywhere on the battlefield, as long as the centre of each is more than 12" from the centre of any other objective marker and more than 6" from the edge of the battlefield.

DEPLOYMENT

The player who placed the sixth objective marker determines which of the standard deployment maps is used in the battle (see the *Warhammer 40,000* rulebook) and picks one of the deployment zones for their army. Their opponent uses the other deployment zone.

The players alternate deploying their units, one at a time, starting with the player who did not pick their deployment zone. A player's models must be set up wholly within their deployment zone. Continue setting up units until both sides have set up their army.

FIRST TURN

The players roll off, and the player who finished setting up their army first adds 1 to their result. The winner can choose to take the first or second turn. If they take the first turn, their opponent can roll a D6; on a 6, they manage to seize the initiative, and they get the first turn instead!

BATTLE LENGTH

At the end of battle round 5, the player who had the first turn rolls a D6. On a 3+, the game continues, otherwise the game is over. At the end of battle round 6, the player who had the second turn rolls a D6. This time the game continues on a 4+, otherwise the game is over. The battle automatically ends at the end of battle round 7.

VICTORY CONDITIONS

At the end of the game, the player with the most victory points is the winner. If both players have the same, the game is a draw. Victory points are scored for the following:

Control or Raze: Each player scores 1 victory point at the end of each of their turns for each objective marker they control. A player controls an objective marker if they have more models within 3" of the centre of it than their opponent does. However, if an objective marker is within the enemy's deployment zone you can choose to raze it if you control it; doing so scores you D3 victory points instead of 1 but that objective marker is then removed from the battlefield.

Slay the Warlord: If the enemy Warlord has been slain during the battle, you score 1 victory point.

First Blood: The first unit, of any kind, to be destroyed during the battle is worth 1 victory point to the opposing player at the end of the game. If two or more units from opposing forces are destroyed simultaneously, then both players get 1 victory point.

Linebreaker: If, at the end of the battle, you have at least one model within the enemy's deployment zone, you score 1 victory point.

+++

TRUE VICTORY LIES NOT IN MERCY, BUT IN THE WHOLESALE ERADICATION OF YOUR FOE.

+++

ETERNAL WAR
DOMINATE AND DESTROY

Sometimes it is not enough simply to defeat your enemy. Rather, you must humble them utterly, seizing control of the battlefield as though it is yours by right and smashing any foe foolish enough to challenge your claim.

THE ARMIES

Each player selects a Battle-forged army to an agreed points limit.

THE BATTLEFIELD

Create the battlefield and set up terrain. Next, the players place six objective markers as follows. The players roll off and, starting with the winner, the players alternate placing these objective markers until all six have been set up. The objective markers can be placed anywhere on the battlefield, as long as the centre of each is more than 12" from the centre of any other objective marker and more than 6" from the edge of the battlefield.

DEPLOYMENT

The player who placed the sixth objective marker determines which of the standard deployment maps is used in the battle (see the *Warhammer 40,000* rulebook) and picks one of the deployment zones for their army. Their opponent uses the other deployment zone.

The players alternate deploying their units, one at a time, starting with the player who did not pick their deployment zone. A player's models must be set up wholly within their deployment zone. Continue setting up units until both sides have set up their army.

FIRST TURN

The players roll off, and the player who finished setting up their army first adds 1 to their result. The winner can choose to take the first or second turn. If they take the first turn, their opponent can roll a D6; on a 6, they manage to seize the initiative, and they get the first turn instead!

BATTLE LENGTH

At the end of battle round 5, the player who had the first turn rolls a D6. On a 3+, the game continues, otherwise the game is over. At the end of battle round 6, the player who had the second turn rolls a D6. This time the game continues on a 4+, otherwise the game is over. The battle automatically ends at the end of battle round 7.

VICTORY CONDITIONS

At the end of the game, the player with the most victory points is the winner. If both players have the same, the game is a draw. Victory points are scored for the following:

Dominate the Battlefield: Each player scores 1 victory point at the end of each of their turns for each objective marker they control. A player controls an objective marker if they have more models within 3" of the centre of it than their opponent does.

No Quarter Given: Each player scores 1 victory point for each enemy unit that is destroyed.

Slay the Warlord: If the enemy Warlord has been slain during the battle, you score 1 victory point. This is in addition to the 1 victory point you score for each destroyed enemy unit.

First Blood: The first unit, of any kind, to be destroyed during the battle is worth 1 victory point to the opposing player at the end of the game. If two or more units from opposing forces are destroyed simultaneously, then both players get 1 victory point.

Linebreaker: If, at the end of the battle, you have at least one model within the enemy's deployment zone, you score 1 victory point.

+++

TODAY'S BUTCHERED FRIEND CANNOT BECOME TOMORROW'S HIDDEN FOE.

+++

ETERNAL WAR
ASCENSION

You have learned of several vital locations where objects that grant great power can be acquired. The leaders of your army must seize this resource, while ensuring it is denied to the enemy's own champions.

+++

THERE ARE GREATER GLORIES TO BE KNOWN IN THIS STRANGE AGE THAN THE SIMPLE TRIUMPH OF VICTORY.

+++

THE ARMIES
Each player selects a Battle-forged army to an agreed points limit.

THE BATTLEFIELD
Create the battlefield and set up terrain.

The players roll off and the winner determines which of the standard deployment maps is used in the battle (see the *Warhammer 40,000* rulebook) and picks one of the deployment zones for their army. Their opponent uses the other deployment zone.

The players then place three objective markers on the battlefield as follows. The first objective marker is set up at the centre of the battlefield. Then, starting with the player who determined the deployment map, the players each place one more objective marker; these can be set up anywhere on the battlefield so long as the centre of the marker is exactly 18" from the centre of the battlefield, at least 12" from both players' deployment zones and more than 12" from the centre of any other objective marker.

DEPLOYMENT
The players alternate deploying their units, one at a time, starting with the player who placed the third objective marker. A player's models must be set up wholly within their deployment zone. Continue setting up units until both sides have set up their army.

FIRST TURN
The players roll off, and the player who finished setting up their army first adds 1 to their result. The winner can choose to take the first or second turn. If they take the first turn, their opponent can roll a D6; on a 6, they manage to seize the initiative, and they get the first turn instead!

BATTLE LENGTH
At the end of battle round 5, the player who had the first turn rolls a D6. On a 3+, the game continues, otherwise the game is over.

At the end of battle round 6, the player who had the second turn rolls a D6. This time the game continues on a 4+, otherwise the game is over. The battle automatically ends at the end of battle round 7.

VICTORY CONDITIONS
At the end of the game, the player with the most victory points is the winner. If both players have the same, the game is a draw. Victory points are scored for the following:

Ascend: Each player scores 1 victory point at the end of each of their turns for each objective marker they control. A player controls an objective marker if they have more models within 3" of the centre of it than their opponent does. However, if only one player has any **CHARACTERS** within 3" of the centre of an objective marker, they control it regardless of the number of nearby enemy models. Furthermore, if a character controls the same objective marker for more than one of their turns consecutively, the number of victory points scored is increased; score 2 victory points at the end of your turn for an objective marker that has been controlled by the character for two of their turns consecutively, 3 victory points if it has been controlled by the character for three of their turns consecutively and so on.

Slay the Warlord: If the enemy Warlord has been slain during the battle, you score 1 victory point.

First Blood: The first unit, of any kind, to be destroyed during the battle is worth 1 victory point to the opposing player at the end of the game. If two or more units from opposing forces are destroyed simultaneously, then both players get 1 victory point.

Linebreaker: If, at the end of the battle, you have at least one model within the enemy's deployment zone, you score 1 victory point.

ETERNAL WAR
ROVING PATROL

Pushing forward through no-man's-land, your advance elements have identified crucial battlefield assets and begun the fight to seize them from the foe. With both forces pouring their reserves into the battle, it will escalate quickly…

THE ARMIES

Each player selects a Battle-forged army to an agreed points limit. Each then divides their army into three forces, with as equal a number of units in each as possible, before rolling a D3 to randomly select one. This is the player's Starting Force. If a player has less than three units, randomly select a unit to be the Starting Force.

THE BATTLEFIELD

Create the battlefield and set up terrain. The players roll off and the winner determines which of the standard deployment maps is used in the battle (see the *Warhammer 40,000* rulebook) and picks one of the deployment zones for their army. Their opponent uses the other deployment zone. The players place 1 objective marker at the centre of the battlefield. Then, starting with the player who determined the deployment map, they each place one more objective marker in their deployment zone and more than 6" from any battlefield edge.

DEPLOYMENT

The players alternate deploying their Starting Force units, one at a time, starting with the player who placed the third objective. Their other units are not set up at the start of the battle. A player's models must be set up wholly within their deployment zone. Continue setting up units until both sides have set up.

FIRST TURN

The players roll off, and the player who finished setting up their army first adds 1 to their result. The winner can choose to take the first or second turn. If they take the first turn, their opponent can roll a D6; on a 6, they manage to seize the initiative, and they get the first turn instead!

RESERVE FORCES

Any unit not set up at the start of the battle starts the game in Reserve. At the end of your first Movement phase, roll a D6 for each of your units in Reserve. On a 3+ that unit is set up wholly within your deployment zone and wholly within 6" of any battlefield edge (units with abilities such as 'Teleport Strike' that allow them to arrive elsewhere may use these). If a unit is embarked within a **TRANSPORT**, they will arrive when their transport does (make one roll for the transport and the units inside). At the end of your second Movement phase, all of your units still in Reserve automatically arrive, and are set up as described above.

BATTLE LENGTH

At the end of battle round 5, the player who had the first turn rolls a D6. On a 3+, the game continues, otherwise the game is over. At the end of battle round 6, the player who had the second turn rolls a D6. This time the game continues on a 4+, otherwise the game is over. The battle automatically ends at the end of battle round 7.

VICTORY CONDITIONS

At the end of the game, the player with the most victory points is the winner. If both players have the same, the game is a draw. Victory points are scored for the following:

Take and Hold: At the end of the game, each objective marker is worth 3 victory points to the player who controls it. A player controls an objective marker if they have more models within 3" of the centre of it than their opponent does.

Slay the Warlord: If the enemy Warlord has been slain during the battle, you score 1 victory point.

First Blood: The first unit, of any kind, to be destroyed during the battle is worth 1 victory point to the opposing player at the end of the game. If two or more units from opposing forces are destroyed simultaneously, then both players get 1 victory point.

Linebreaker: If, at the end of the battle, you have at least one model within the enemy's deployment zone, you score 1 victory point.

+++

NO BATTLE IS TOO COSTLY, NOR BUTCHER'S BILL TOO HIGH, THAT BRINGS VICTORY OVER A HATED FOE.

+++

KILL CONFIRMED

Amidst the madness of battle, the order comes through: the enemy's forces must be eliminated at all costs. You must spare no effort in neutralising your foe's warriors as quickly as you can, for they are trying to do the same thing to you.

THE ARMIES

Each player selects a Battle-forged army to an agreed points limit.

THE BATTLEFIELD

Create the battlefield and set up terrain. The players place six objective markers, as detailed in the Tactical Objectives section of the *Warhammer 40,000* rulebook.

DEPLOYMENT

The player who placed the sixth objective marker determines which of the standard deployment maps is used in the battle (see the *Warhammer 40,000* rulebook) and picks one of the deployment zones for their army. Their opponent uses the other deployment zone.

The players alternate deploying their units, one at a time, starting with the player who did not pick their deployment zone. A player's models must be set up wholly within their deployment zone. Continue setting up units until both sides have set up their army.

FIRST TURN

The players roll off, and the player who finished setting up their army first adds 1 to their result. The winner can choose to take the first or second turn. If they take the first turn, their opponent can roll a D6; on a 6, they manage to seize the initiative, and they get the first turn instead!

TACTICAL OBJECTIVES

This mission uses Tactical Objectives. If, at the start of a player's turn, they have fewer than 3 active Tactical Objectives, they must generate Tactical Objectives until they have 3.

KILL ORDER

In this mission, Tactical Objectives that are achieved when an enemy unit is destroyed can only be discarded when they are achieved, unless they are impossible to achieve (e.g. if you generated 'Witch Hunter', but your opponent no longer has any PSYKERS left in their army, you can choose to discard it at the end of your turn in the usual way).

BATTLE LENGTH

At the end of battle round 5, the player who had the first turn rolls a D6. On a 3+, the game continues, otherwise the game is over. At the end of battle round 6, the player who had the second turn rolls a D6. This time the game continues on a 4+, otherwise the game is over. The battle automatically ends at the end of battle round 7.

VICTORY CONDITIONS

At the end of the game, the player with the most victory points is the winner. If both players have the same, the game is a draw. In addition to achieving Tactical Objectives, victory points are scored for the following:

No Quarter Given: Each player scores 1 victory point for each enemy unit that is destroyed.

Slay the Warlord: If the enemy Warlord has been slain during the battle, you score 1 victory point. This is in addition to the 1 victory point you score for each destroyed enemy unit.

First Blood: The first unit, of any kind, to be destroyed during the battle is worth 1 victory point to the opposing player at the end of the game. If two or more units from opposing forces are destroyed simultaneously, then both players get 1 victory point.

Linebreaker: If, at the end of the battle, you have at least one model within the enemy's deployment zone, you score 1 victory point.

MAELSTROM OF WAR
TARGETS OF OPPORTUNITY

At the battle's bleeding edge, you alone can seize the split-second opportunities that make the difference between victory and defeat. You must out-manoeuvre and out-think your enemy, and snatch victory out of their very hands.

THE ARMIES

Each player selects a Battle-forged army to an agreed points limit.

THE BATTLEFIELD

Create the battlefield and set up terrain. The players place six objective markers, as detailed in the Tactical Objectives section of the *Warhammer 40,000* rulebook.

DEPLOYMENT

The player who placed the sixth objective marker determines which of the standard deployment maps is used in the battle (see the *Warhammer 40,000* rulebook) and picks one of the deployment zones for their army. Their opponent uses the other deployment zone. The players alternate deploying their units, one at a time, starting with the player who did not pick their deployment zone. A player's models must be set up wholly within their deployment zone. Continue setting up units until both sides have set up their army.

FIRST TURN

The players roll off, and the player who finished setting up their army first adds 1 to their result. The winner can choose to take the first or second turn. If they take the first turn, their opponent can roll a D6; on a 6, they manage to seize the initiative, and they get the first turn instead!

TACTICAL OBJECTIVES

This mission uses Tactical Objectives. At the start of a player's turn, after discarding all active Tactical Objectives as described in the Opportunity Lost rule below, they generate 3 new Tactical Objectives.

OPPORTUNITY LOST

At the start of each player's turn, before generating new Tactical Objectives, all of their remaining active Tactical Objectives are discarded – the window of opportunity to achieve these has been lost. This essentially means that a player only has a single turn to achieve any Tactical Objective they generate.

STRATAGEM

In this mission, players can spend Command Points (CPs) to use the following Stratagem:

2CP

SECOND CHANCE
Maelstrom of War Stratagem

Use this Stratagem at the start of your turn, before discarding your Tactical Objectives. Select one active Tactical Objective; that one will not be discarded due to the Opportunity Lost rule. You still generate 3 new ones after the others have been discarded (for a total of 4).

BATTLE LENGTH

At the end of battle round 5, the player who had the first turn rolls a D6. On a 3+, the game continues, otherwise the game is over. At the end of battle round 6, the player who had the second turn rolls a D6. This time the game continues on a 4+, otherwise the game is over. The battle automatically ends at the end of battle round 7.

VICTORY CONDITIONS

At the end of the game, the player with the most victory points is the winner. If both players have the same, the game is a draw. In addition to achieving Tactical Objectives, victory points are scored for the following:

Slay the Warlord: If the enemy Warlord has been slain during the battle, you score 1 victory point.

First Blood: The first unit, of any kind, to be destroyed during the battle is worth 1 victory point to the opposing player at the end of the game. If two or more units from opposing forces are destroyed simultaneously, then both players get 1 victory point.

Linebreaker: If, at the end of the battle, you have at least one model within the enemy's deployment zone, you score 1 victory point.

+++

HOPE IS THE OPIATE OF THE WEAKLING AND THE FOOL. THE FAITHFUL MAN NEEDS NO SUCH EMPTY PROMISES.

+++

MAELSTROM OF WAR
TACTICAL GAMBIT

Sometimes, victory goes to the commander most willing to take a big risk, and most able to see it through to a successful conclusion. You must now do both, while ensuring that you sabotage your enemy's attempts to do the same.

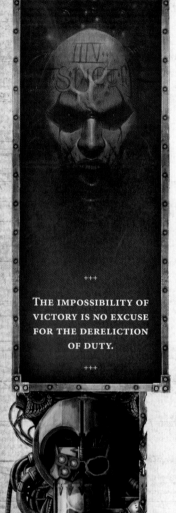

THE IMPOSSIBILITY OF VICTORY IS NO EXCUSE FOR THE DERELICTION OF DUTY.

THE ARMIES

Each player selects a Battle-forged army to an agreed points limit.

THE BATTLEFIELD

Create the battlefield and set up terrain. The players place six objective markers, as detailed in the Tactical Objectives section of the *Warhammer 40,000* rulebook.

DEPLOYMENT

The player who placed the sixth objective marker determines which of the standard deployment maps is used in the battle (see the *Warhammer 40,000* rulebook) and picks one of the deployment zones for their army. Their opponent uses the other deployment zone. The players alternate deploying their units, one at a time, starting with the player who did not pick their deployment zone. A player's models must be set up wholly within their deployment zone. Continue setting up units until both sides have set up their army.

FIRST TURN

The players roll off, and the player who finished setting up their army first adds 1 to their result. The winner can choose to take the first or second turn. If they take the first turn, their opponent can roll a D6; on a 6, they manage to seize the initiative, and they get the first turn instead!

THE GAMBIT

At the start of each player's turn, before generating new Tactical Objectives (see below), the player must declare how many they think they can achieve before the start of their next turn: 1, 2, 3 or 4 (you cannot declare 0).

TACTICAL OBJECTIVES

This mission uses Tactical Objectives. If, at the start of a player's turn, they have fewer than 4 active Tactical Objectives, they must generate Tactical Objectives until they have 4. Players must not generate new Tactical Objectives until after they have declared their gambit for this turn, as described above.

BATTLE LENGTH

At the end of battle round 5, the player who had the first turn rolls a D6. On a 3+, the game continues, otherwise the game is over. At the end of battle round 6, the player who had the second turn rolls a D6. This time the game continues on a 4+, otherwise the game is over. The battle automatically ends at the end of battle round 7.

VICTORY CONDITIONS

At the end of the game, the player with the most victory points is the winner. If both players have the same, the game is a draw. In addition to achieving Tactical Objectives, victory points are scored for the following:

Bold Gamble: At the end of each player's turn, that player must count how many Tactical Objectives they achieved during their turn and compare it to the number they declared they would achieve at the start of the turn. If they have achieved at least that many Tactical Objectives, they score a number of victory points equal to the number they declared. If they achieved less, however, their opponent scores that many victory points. Note that Tactical Objectives achieved during your opponent's turn do not count towards the total for your turn (you still score the Victory Points awarded by the Tactical Objective itself, but they can't help you achieve your gambit for the turn).

Slay the Warlord: If the enemy Warlord has been slain during the battle, you score 1 victory point.

First Blood: The first unit, of any kind, to be destroyed during the battle is worth 1 victory point to the opposing player at the end of the game. If two or more units from opposing forces are destroyed simultaneously, then both players get 1 victory point.

Linebreaker: If, at the end of the battle, you have at least one model within the enemy's deployment zone, you score 1 victory point.

MAELSTROM OF WAR
RACE TO VICTORY

Doom approaches, and you must seize victory before it descends. A plummeting meteorite, an onrushing swarm or the detonation of a viral warhead; whatever the threat, you must beat it – and your opponent – to the punch.

THE ARMIES
Each player selects a Battle-forged army to an agreed points limit.

THE BATTLEFIELD
Create the battlefield and set up terrain. The players place six objective markers, as detailed in the Tactical Objectives section of the *Warhammer 40,000* rulebook.

DEPLOYMENT
The player who placed the sixth objective marker determines which of the standard deployment maps is used in the battle (see the *Warhammer 40,000* rulebook) and picks one of the deployment zones for their army. Their opponent uses the other deployment zone.

The players alternate deploying their units, one at a time, starting with the player who did not pick their deployment zone. A player's models must be set up wholly within their deployment zone. Continue setting up units until both sides have set up their army.

FIRST TURN
The players roll off, and the player who finished setting up their army first adds 1 to their result. The winner can choose to take the first or second turn. If they take the first turn, their opponent can roll a D6; on a 6, they manage to seize the initiative, and they get the first turn instead!

TACTICAL OBJECTIVES
This mission uses Tactical Objectives. If, at the start of a player's turn, they have fewer than 3 active Tactical Objectives, they must generate Tactical Objectives until they have 3.

BATTLE LENGTH
In this mission, the players are attempting to achieving 10 Tactical Objectives before their opponent. The game ends at the end of the battle round in which either player has achieved 10 or more Tactical Objectives.

Otherwise, at the end of battle round 5, the player who had the first turn rolls a D6. On a 3+, the game continues, otherwise the game is over, even if neither player has achieved 10 Tactical Objectives. At the end of battle round 6, the player who had the second turn rolls a D6. This time the game continues on a 4+, otherwise the game is over, even if neither player has achieved 10 Tactical Objectives. The battle automatically ends at the end of battle round 7, regardless of how many Tactical Objectives have been achieved.

Designer's Note: *The target of 10 Tactical Objectives assumes that players are using armies with a points limit between 1,001 and 2,000. If the points limit is less than this, reduce the target to 8 Tactical Objectives. If it is more, increase it to 12.*

VICTORY CONDITIONS
At the end of the game, the player with the most victory points is the winner. If both players have the same, the game is a draw. In addition to achieving Tactical Objectives, victory points are scored for the following:

Glory to the First: The first player to achieve their tenth Tactical Objective scores 3 victory points.

Slay the Warlord: If the enemy Warlord has been slain during the battle, you score 1 victory point.

First Blood: The first unit, of any kind, to be destroyed during the battle is worth 1 victory point to the opposing player at the end of the game. If two or more units from opposing forces are destroyed simultaneously, then both players get 1 victory point.

Linebreaker: If, at the end of the battle, you have at least one model within the enemy's deployment zone, you score 1 victory point.

+++

NO AMOUNT OF
PLANNING AND
FORETHOUGHT CAN
COUNTER SUFFICIENT
BELLIGERENT ZEAL.

+++

MAELSTROM OF WAR
SEALED ORDERS

You face a true strategic challenge. With your orders filtering through in coded parcels, and only your success unlocking the next part of the plan, you must achieve your objectives at all costs or be left as a failure in the dust of the battlefield.

THE ARMIES

Each player selects a Battle-forged army to an agreed points limit.

THE BATTLEFIELD

Create the battlefield and set up terrain. The players place six objective markers, as detailed in the Tactical Objectives section of the *Warhammer 40,000* rulebook.

DEPLOYMENT

The player who placed the sixth objective marker determines which of the standard deployment maps is used in the battle (see the *Warhammer 40,000* rulebook) and picks one of the deployment zones for their army. Their opponent uses the other deployment zone. The players alternate deploying their units, one at a time, starting with the player who did not pick their deployment zone. A player's models must be set up wholly within their deployment zone. Continue setting up units until both sides have set up their army.

FIRST TURN

The players roll off, and the player who finished setting up their army first adds 1 to their result. The winner can choose to take the first or second turn. If they take the first turn, their opponent can roll a D6; on a 6, they manage to seize the initiative, and they get the first turn instead!

TACTICAL OBJECTIVES

This mission uses Tactical Objectives. At the start of each player's first turn, they generate 6 Tactical Objectives. If, at the start of a player's subsequent turn, they have no active Tactical Objectives remaining, they must generate new Tactical Objectives. The first time a player runs out of Tactical Objectives they generate 5 new ones. The second time they run out they generate 4 new ones, and so on.

SECRET ORDERS

In this mission, players keep their Tactical Objectives secret from each other. Only reveal Tactical Objectives when achieving them.

BATTLE LENGTH

At the end of battle round 5, the player who had the first turn rolls a D6. On a 3+, the game continues, otherwise the game is over. At the end of battle round 6, the player who had the second turn rolls a D6. This time the game continues on a 4+, otherwise the game is over. The battle automatically ends at the end of battle round 7.

STRATAGEM

In this mission, players can spend Command Points (CPs) to use the following Stratagem:

1CP

ACCEPTABLE LOSSES
Maelstrom of War Stratagem
Use this Stratagem at the end of your turn to discard up to 3 of your active Tactical Objectives.

VICTORY CONDITIONS

At the end of the game, the player with the most victory points is the winner. If both players have the same, the game is a draw. In addition to achieving Tactical Objectives, victory points are scored for the following:

Slay the Warlord: If the enemy Warlord has been slain during the battle, you score 1 victory point.

First Blood: The first unit, of any kind, to be destroyed during the battle is worth 1 victory point to the opposing player at the end of the game. If two or more units from opposing forces are destroyed simultaneously, then both players get 1 victory point.

Linebreaker: If, at the end of the battle, you have at least one model within the enemy's deployment zone, you score 1 victory point.

+++

ASK NOT WHY YOU MUST SERVE. ASK NOT HOW. ASK ONLY FOR THE CHANCE TO DO SO, AND TO DIE AT DUTY'S END.

+++

MAELSTROM OF WAR
RECON

While moving through no-man's-land, you have located a site of surprising strategic importance. Reinforcements are rushing to help you claim this prize for yourself, but your enemy is striving just as hard to rip it from your grasp.

THE ARMIES

Each player selects a Battle-forged army to an agreed points limit. Each then divides their army into three forces, with as equal a number of units in each as possible, before rolling a D3 to randomly select one. This is the player's Starting Force. If a player has less than three units, randomly select a unit to be the Starting Force.

THE BATTLEFIELD

Create the battlefield and set up terrain. The players place six objective markers, as detailed in the Tactical Objectives section of the *Warhammer 40,000* rulebook.

DEPLOYMENT

The player who placed the sixth objective marker determines which of the standard deployment maps is used in the battle (see the *Warhammer 40,000* rulebook) and picks one of the deployment zones for their army. Their opponent uses the other deployment zone.

The players alternate deploying their Starting Force units, one at a time, starting with the player who did not pick their deployment zone. Their other units are not set up at the start of the battle. A player's models must be set up wholly within their deployment zone. Continue setting up units until both sides have set up.

FIRST TURN

The players roll off, and the player who finished setting up their army first adds 1 to their result. The winner can choose to take the first or second turn. If they take the first turn, their opponent can roll a D6; on a 6, they manage to seize the initiative, and they get the first turn instead!

TACTICAL OBJECTIVES

This mission uses Tactical Objectives. If, at the start of a player's turn, they have fewer than 3 active Tactical Objectives, they must generate Tactical Objectives until they have 3.

RESERVE FORCES

Any unit not set up at the start of the battle starts the game in Reserve. At the end of your first Movement phase, roll a D6 for each of your units in Reserve. On a 3+ that unit is set up wholly within your deployment zone and wholly within 6" of any battlefield edge (units with abilities such as 'Teleport Strike' that allow them to arrive elsewhere may use these). If a unit is embarked within a **Transport**, they will arrive when their transport does (make one roll for the transport and the units inside). At the end of your second Movement phase, all of your units still in Reserve automatically arrive, and are set up as described above.

BATTLE LENGTH

At the end of battle round 5, the player who had the first turn rolls a D6. On a 3+, the game continues, otherwise the game is over. At the end of battle round 6, the player who had the second turn rolls a D6. This time the game continues on a 4+, otherwise the game is over. The battle automatically ends at the end of battle round 7.

VICTORY CONDITIONS

At the end of the game, the player with the most victory points is the winner. If both players have the same, the game is a draw. In addition to achieving Tactical Objectives, victory points are scored for the following:

Slay the Warlord: If the enemy Warlord has been slain during the battle, you score 1 victory point.

First Blood: The first unit, of any kind, to be destroyed during the battle is worth 1 victory point to the opposing player at the end of the game. If two or more units from opposing forces are destroyed simultaneously, then both players get 1 victory point.

Linebreaker: If, at the end of the battle, you have at least one model within the enemy's deployment zone, you score 1 victory point.

+++

THE FAITHFUL WARRIOR NEEDS NO REWARD EXCEPT FOR AN ENDLESS SUPPLY OF FOES TO VANQUISH.

+++

OBJECTIVE MARKERS

A common theme in many matched play battles is the capturing of objectives. These can represent all manner of valuable assets, from crucial strategic locations or valuable materiel to enemy spies, ancient relics, terrified dignitaries, top-secret plans, or whatever else your imagination can conceive of.

Warhammer 40,000 armies look fantastic on the tabletop. From towering monsters to lumbering war engines, massed infantry to hurtling combat aircraft and more, they present a magnificent spectacle. A well-presented battlefield further elevates this visual grandeur, with painted and evocative scenery pieces for your armies to battle in and around.

But what about the prizes you are fighting over? Objectives on the battlefield can be represented with any token or counter you choose. But, just as a bare tabletop with some books piled on it for hills can't compare with a shattered worldscape covered in gothic ruins and alien jungle, rudimentary objective markers just aren't as evocative or exciting as something a little more elaborate.

Many players therefore enjoy the modelling challenge of creating their own objective markers. These can be as simple or as complex as you like, and while some people prefer generic objective markers that can be applicable to any gaming table or environment, others prefer to craft themed markers that go with their army and increase its presence on the tabletop.

Good examples of simple and generic markers would be things like crates, barrels and containers. Perhaps they hold ammunition supplies or vital power cells? Maybe they're containers of gene-seed stolen from a Space Marine Chapter's precious reserves? They could contain the plans for an anti-Tyranid bio-weapon or a series of blasphemous tomes of lore crucial for Daemon-summoning rituals. The list goes on, with the very neutrality of such simple markers allowing for whatever interpretation players desire of their contents.

Even with such straightforward objective markers, there are certain basic steps that you may want to take to ensure they look their best, and are at their most useful on the tabletop.

Painting

Always put as much time and effort into painting your objective markers as you would into other models that you're planning to put on the tabletop. A lot of generic objective markers are likely to be quite straightforward-looking objects, so they may not take a whole lot of work to get to a good standard, but it's still worth taking the time to undercoat, base, wash, layer and highlight them. Doing this will tie them properly into the environment around them. Some of the Citadel Paint System's Technical paints are especially useful for making objective markers look great with minimum effort. Corroded relics, sacrificial altars sprayed with blood, and the glowing lenses of shield generators are all effects that look great on the tabletop.

Bases

Whether a heap of shattered helmets or a stack of ammo crates, it's always best to put your objective markers onto a suitably sized base. 25mm bases will suffice, but to make them really stand out, a 40mm base is definitely the best size.

Numbering

Numbering your markers in some manner is also a good idea. There are many missions, both in Eternal War and Maelstrom of War, where this is an important consideration. You can simply paint the numbers 1 to 6 on the objective's base, but it's a lot more fun to find some in-world method of identifying them – such as painting Imperial gothic numerals onto the sides of crates and barrels, attaching a certain number of glowing lights or lenses, or affixing the appropriate amount of skulls to a spike. However you choose to do it, this sort of additional creative step takes very little extra work but looks great in-game.

Theme

Beyond simply constructing basic objective markers, many gamers enjoy fashioning a set that are themed to a specific battlefield. This is actually very easy to do. Anyone who has been building up the same army for any length of time will usually find themselves with plenty of spare bits and pieces left over from the Citadel Miniatures kits they've built. Whether this be spare shoulder pads or weapons, unused back banners, skull piles or trophies, such things can make fantastic themed objective markers.

It's worth ensuring that whatever components you choose are suitable. Have a think before reaching for your clippers – are the bits you've found big enough to make impressive, easily visible objective markers? Do you have enough to make a full set of six markers? While a single Space Marine helm might seem cool at first glance, in reality it's going to get lost on the battlefield, even if it's stuck to a base. On the other hand, a heap of severed helms piled up or impaled on spikes would make for a marvellous Chaos Space Marine objective marker, and a set of six, each modelled slightly differently, would look even better.

For inspiration, look no further than your army's codex, or any of the myriad pieces of grim and gothic artwork scattered throughout Warhammer 40,000 publications. If you have a Space Wolves army, for example, you could create six banner poles jutting from the snow-covered ground, hung with wolf-tail talismans and covered in runes. For an Astra Militarum player, numbered hovering servo-skulls, piles of spare weapons and ammo, or small shrines to the Emperor would be ideal. Tyranid players could craft scuttling brain-beasts to be devoured, while Necron players may want to mark out the numerals on their objectives with scarabs, and T'au collectors may wish to lace the battlefield with hovering spy-drones that need to be snatched up before the enemy can destroy them.

Whatever you decide to do, with a bit of time and effort you will create something exciting and unique that will make a great addition to your games and your army. On the following pages, you will find details of some objective markers we have made for *Chapter Approved*. Have a go at making some of them, or use them as inspiration for your own designs.

SPACE MARINES OBJECTIVE MARKERS

SECURED FOR THE EMPEROR

The objective markers shown below are from the Sector Imperialis Objectives set, and are ideal for use with a Space Marines collection. The Emperor's finest are typically sent to secure the most crucial of battlefield targets, which these markers represent very well. From the doomsday bomb that could destroy a world, to the xenos specimen that cannot fall into enemy hands, and the crashed saviour pod that bore a Planetary Governor to safety, these markers not only reflect the vital nature of the Space Marines' targets, but contribute to the narrative of the game that you are playing.

IMPERIAL OBJECTIVE MARKERS

WORLDS OF THE IMPERIUM

The objective markers shown here were made using the Warhammer 40,000 Hero Bases set, and tie well into the aesthetic of Imperial armies, from unexploded munitions to secret bunker entrances. Note also the numbering on these markers that helps them function in their in-game capacity.

VITAL SUPPLIES

Crates, barrels and bits of equipment make for excellent Imperium-themed objective markers. These were made using the Battlefield Accessories Set combined with spare bits from Space Marines vehicle kits. They are ideal for missions that involve capturing supplies and munitions, and are easy to adorn with numerals for identification.

CHAOS OBJECTIVE MARKERS

FOR THE DARK GODS!

These objective markers were made using spare components from plastic Chaos Space Marines kits.

In keeping with the cruel nature of the Heretic Astartes, they are numbered by the amount of spikes that jut from them.

NECRON OBJECTIVE MARKERS

THE SLUMBERING DEAD

These objective markers were made using spare Necron Warriors left over from building an Annihilation Barge.

The scarabs arranged on the bases of these skeletal Necron statuettes indicate the number of each objective marker.

TYRANID OBJECTIVE MARKERS

TWISTED LIFEFORMS

These objective markers were made using spare plastic components from Tyranid sprues, and represent the vile bioforms that infest any world the Tyranids invade.

DRUKHARI OBJECTIVE MARKERS

POISONED PRIZES

These objective markers were made using spare plastic Drukhari components, and evoke the cruel aesthetic of the Commorrite raiders.

The number of skulls adorning these grim monuments denotes the numerical designation of each marker.

T'AU EMPIRE OBJECTIVE MARKERS

FOR THE GREATER GOOD

These objective markers represent fallen Drones loaded with vital tactical intelligence. They are made from plastic spare parts from T'au Empire kits.

Each Drone is marked with a T'au numeral that signifies the marker's number.

ORK OBJECTIVE MARKERS

GUBBINZ AND BITZ

These ramshackle Ork objective markers were built using spare parts from plastic Ork sprues.

The objective numbers on these colourful markers have been etched in crude tally-marks by some unusually well-organised Ork Mekaniak.

FACTION RULES

Here you will find additional rules for nearly a dozen different Factions, including Stratagems, abilities, Warlord Traits and psychic powers. Taken together, these better reflect a Faction's unique methods of waging war in the 41st Millennium.

Since the publication of Warhammer 40,000, several codexes have been released, each describing a particular Faction in detail. Each codex provides players with, amongst other things, additional rules that can be used when fielding Detachments of that Faction's units in a Battle-forged army. At the time of writing this book, we are aware that several codex books have yet to be published, and so not all Factions have access to these sorts of rules. This section is therefore designed to give these patient players a set of rules to use in the interim until the codex for their Faction is released.

This section lists additional rules for several specific Factions – **Thousand Sons, Harlequins, Deathwatch, Genestealer Cults, Drukhari, T'au Empire, Adepta Sororitas, Orks, Necrons, Imperial Knights** and **Space Wolves.**

ABILITIES

To use these rules you must have a Battle-forged army. If all of the units in a Detachment have the same Faction keyword, and that keyword is one of those listed above, that Detachment gains the following ability:

Objective Secured

The backbone of any army is the rank and file, the dogged infantry who must consolidate hard-earned ground and hold it in the face of devastating counter-attacks and overwhelming odds.

If your army is Battle-forged, all Troops units in <**Faction**> Detachments gain this ability. Such a unit that is within range of an objective marker (as specified in the mission) controls it even if there are more enemy models within range of it. If an enemy unit within range of the objective marker has a similar ability, then it is controlled by the player who has the most models within range as normal.

WARLORD TRAIT

If a <**Faction**> **Character** is your Warlord, you can generate a Warlord Trait from the appropriate table in this section for them instead of one from the *Warhammer 40,000* rulebook.

RELIC

If your army is led by a <**Faction**> Warlord, then before the battle you may give the appropriate relic from this section to a <**Faction**> **Character** in your army. Named characters such as Magnus the Red, Ghazghkull Thraka and Imotekh the Stormlord cannot be given relics.

Note that some relics replace one of the character's existing weapons. Where this is the case, if you are playing a matched play game or are otherwise using points values, you must still pay the cost of the weapon that is being replaced. Write down any Relics your characters have on your army roster.

STRATAGEMS

If your army is Battle-forged and includes any <**Faction**> Detachments (excluding Auxiliary Support Detachments), you have access to that Faction's Stratagems, meaning you can spend Command Points to activate them. These help to reflect that Faction's preferred tactics and strategies.

PSYCHIC POWERS

Before the battle, a <**Faction**> **Psyker** can choose to replace one of their other psychic powers with the appropriate psychic power listed in this section (you cannot choose to replace the *Smite* psychic power).

KEYWORDS

Throughout this section you will come across keywords that are within angular brackets, such as <**Sept**>. This is shorthand for a keyword of your choice. When including a unit in your army that has a keyword in angular brackets, you must decide which sub-faction it is from and replace that keyword in every instance on its datasheet, and in the rules presented in this section, with your chosen keyword. For example, for a T'au Empire army from Vior'la, <**Sept**> becomes **Vior'la**.

In this section we also refer to the <**Faction**> keyword. This is shorthand for one of the Faction keywords listed on the left. For example, if you have a Detachment of units that uses the **Ork** keyword, the first sentence of the Objective Secured ability would read: 'If your army is Battle-forged, all Troops units in **Ork** Detachments gain this ability.'

ADEPTA SORORITAS

The Adepta Sororitas is the Chamber Militant of the Adeptus Ministorum. It is formed entirely of women, and hence is also known as the Sisterhood. When the Ecclesiarchy declares a War of Faith, it is the Adepta Sororitas that provides its elite forces, slaying the Emperor's enemies without compassion. Indeed, the perfervid nature of the Adepta Sororitas' faith is a potent weapon, manifesting as divine inspiration that drives the Sisters of Battle to feats of martial prowess.

WARLORD TRAIT

If an **ADEPTA SORORITAS CHARACTER** is your Warlord, you can choose to give them the following Warlord Trait:

INSPIRING ORATOR

Those who hear this Warlord's stirring words are inspired to great feats of bravery.

You can re-roll failed Morale tests for friendly **ADEPTA SORORITAS** units within 6" of this Warlord.

RELIC

If your army is led by an **ADEPTA SORORITAS** Warlord, then you may give the following Relic to an **ADEPTA SORORITAS CHARACTER** in your army.

BLADE OF ADMONITION

This blessed power sword is the very blade carried by Alicia Dominica – the founding saint of the Adepta Sororitas – and was famously used to cut the head from the arch-traitor Goge Vandire and bring an end to the Reign of Blood. St. Dominica wielded this blade in the decades following the Ecclesiarchy's reformation, and a thousand more false prophets were slain by its razor edge before Alicia's eventual martyrdom.

Model with a power sword only. The Blade of Admonition replaces the bearer's power sword and has the following profile:

WEAPON	RANGE	TYPE	S	AP	D
Blade of Admonition	Melee	Melee	+2	-3	3

STRATAGEMS

If your army is Battle-forged and includes any **ADEPTA SORORITAS** Detachments (excluding Auxiliary Support Detachments), you have access to the following Stratagems:

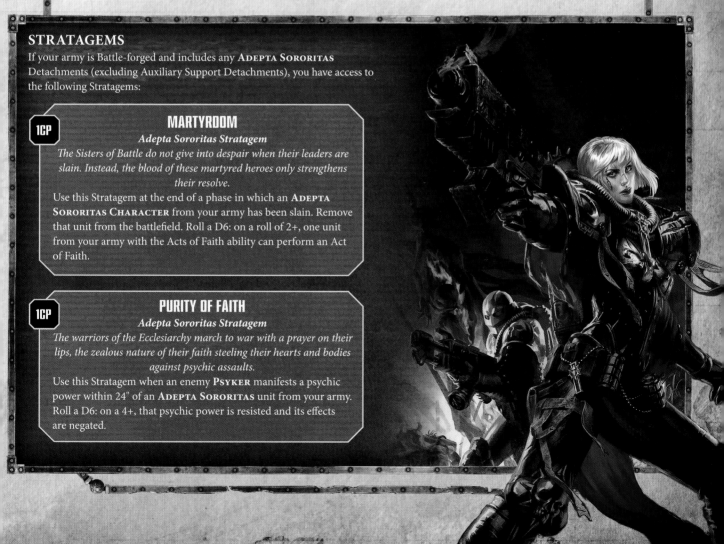

1CP

MARTYRDOM
Adepta Sororitas Stratagem

The Sisters of Battle do not give into despair when their leaders are slain. Instead, the blood of these martyred heroes only strengthens their resolve.

Use this Stratagem at the end of a phase in which an **ADEPTA SORORITAS CHARACTER** from your army has been slain. Remove that unit from the battlefield. Roll a D6: on a roll of 2+, one unit from your army with the Acts of Faith ability can perform an Act of Faith.

1CP

PURITY OF FAITH
Adepta Sororitas Stratagem

The warriors of the Ecclesiarchy march to war with a prayer on their lips, the zealous nature of their faith steeling their hearts and bodies against psychic assaults.

Use this Stratagem when an enemy **PSYKER** manifests a psychic power within 24" of an **ADEPTA SORORITAS** unit from your army. Roll a D6: on a 4+, that psychic power is resisted and its effects are negated.

DEATHWATCH

The battle-brothers of the Deathwatch are the foremost xenos hunters in the Imperium. They are a black-clad brotherhood of warriors, bound by ancient oaths to defend Mankind from the alien, no matter its form. Hand-picked from the breadth of the Adeptus Astartes for their expertise in the slaughter of xenos threats, each of those who have joined the Long Vigil is a hero, tempered in the furnace of conflict and girded for battle with an arsenal of specialist weaponry.

WARLORD TRAIT

If a **DEATHWATCH CHARACTER** is your Warlord, you can choose to give them the following Warlord Trait:

BANE OF MONSTROSITIES

This Warlord specialises in bringing down those behemoths that anchor the centre of the xenos warhost.

You can re-roll failed wound rolls for your Warlord when attacking enemy **VEHICLES** or **MONSTERS**.

RELIC

If your army is led by a **DEATHWATCH** Warlord, then you may give the following Relic to a **DEATHWATCH CHARACTER** in your army.

THE BEACON ANGELIS

The Beacon Angelis was devised to guide the Deathwatch to the threshold of the alien adversary. Housed within a reliquary, it calls out to the augur arrays of the Deathwatch with the voices of a hundred electric cherubim. Its summons is so strong that it will draw the righteous unto its locale regardless of what darkness may surround it.

Once per battle, at the end of any of your Movement phases, the bearer can use the Beacon Angelis to teleport a unit to his position. When he does so, select a friendly **DEATHWATCH INFANTRY** or **BIKER** unit that is either on the battlefield, or is in a teleportarium. In either case, remove this unit and then set it up wholly within 6" of the bearer and more than 9" from any enemy model (any model that cannot be set up is slain).

STRATAGEMS

If your army is Battle-forged and includes any **DEATHWATCH** Detachments (excluding Auxiliary Support Detachments), you have access to the following Stratagems:

1CP

CLAVIS
Deathwatch Stratagem
This rare artefact contains an ancient machine spirit that can disrupt nearby mechanisms.
Use this Stratagem in your Fight phase. Select an enemy **VEHICLE** within 1" of a Watch Master from your army and roll a D6; on a 2+ the vehicle suffers D3 mortal wounds.

1CP

DEATH TO THE ALIEN!
Deathwatch Stratagem
He who allows the alien to live shares its crime of existence.
Use this Stratagem before a **DEATHWATCH** unit from your army is chosen to attack in any Fight phase. Each time you make a hit roll of 6+ for a model in this unit during this phase, it can, if it is targeting a unit that does not have the **IMPERIUM**, **CHAOS** or **UNALIGNED** keyword, immediately make an extra attack against the same unit using the same weapon. These extra attacks cannot themselves generate any further attacks.

DRUKHARI

Piratical raiders who literally feed on pain, the Drukhari are a nightmare made real. From the impossible city of Commorragh hidden deep in the webway, they launch raids all across the galaxy to plunder and enslave the populations of vulnerable worlds, striking hard and fast before vanishing like smoke on the breeze.

Designer's Note: *The following rules cannot be used by any units in a Detachment that contains units with the* **Ynnari** *keyword.*

WARLORD TRAIT

If a **Drukhari Character** is your Warlord, you can choose to give them the appropriate Warlord Trait listed below. <**Wych Cult**> **Characters** (including Lelith Hesperax) can be given the Blood Dancer trait. <**Haemonculus Coven**> **Characters** (including Urien Rakarth) can be given the Master Regenesist trait. All other **Drukhari Characters** can be given the Hatred Eternal trait.

Blood Dancer

A star of the Commorrite arenas, the Warlord excels at close-quarters combat.

Each time you roll a hit roll of 6+ for this Warlord in the Fight phase, that hit causes 3 hits instead of 1.

Master Regenesist

The Haemonculus' flesh regenerates at a frightening rate, pale scar tissue drawing over wounds as if possessed of some sentience.

This Warlord heals D3 lost wounds at the start of each of your turns.

Hatred Eternal

The Warlord is disgusted by the younger races that infest the galaxy, sickened by the unwashed and unrefined multitudes wallowing in their own filth. They will take any opportunity to exterminate such vermin, revelling in every unworthy life they extinguish.

Re-roll hit rolls and wound rolls of 1 for this Warlord in the Fight phase.

RELIC

If your army is led by a **Drukhari** Warlord, then you may give the following Relic to a **Drukhari Character** in your army.

The Parasite's Kiss

Thought to be the finest splinter pistol ever crafted, this weapon spits out crystalline darts bound with psycho-vampiric circuitry. Upon biting into flesh, the target's very soul is leached, and transferred back to the gun's wielder. As the luckless victim withers like rotten fruit, their killer flushes with vigour, revelling in their stolen life energies while their foe crumbles away to dust on the breeze.

Model with a splinter pistol only. The Parasite's Kiss replaces the bearer's splinter pistol and has the following profile:

WEAPON	RANGE	TYPE	S	AP	D
The Parasite's Kiss	12"	Pistol 2	1	-2	2

Abilities: This weapon wounds on a 2+, unless it is targeting a **Vehicle**, in which case it wounds on a 6+. Each time this weapon kills an enemy model, the bearer regains 1 lost wound.

STRATAGEM

If your army is Battle-forged and includes any **Drukhari** Detachments (excluding Auxiliary Support Detachments), you have access to the following Stratagem:

1CP/3CP — WEBWAY PORTAL
Drukhari Stratagem

Appearing as jagged, rune-graven crystals, these devices are hurled into the air before, with a crackle of energy, they tear a rent in the skein of reality, flaying a route into the webway through which the Drukhari can pour.
Use this Stratagem during deployment. If you spend 1 CP, you can set up one **Drukhari Infantry**, **Biker** or **Beasts** unit from your army in the webway instead of placing it on the battlefield. If you spend 3 CPs, you can set up two such units in the webway instead. Units in the webway can emerge at the end of any of your Movement phases – set them up anywhere on the battlefield that is more than 9" from any enemy units. You can only use this Stratagem once per battle.

GENESTEALER CULTS

Amid the blood-chilling shrieks of alien beasts comes the sound of chanting. Thousands of cultist voices are raised in prayer to their Patriarch, a living god from beyond the stars. The skittering shadows in the distance resolve into darting shapes, then a seething tide. A living wave of hybrid creatures boils out from dank and slimy lairs, a menace in numbers enough to conquer a world, as charismatic leaders cast their dominion over the foe. The cult has prepared long for this day of reckoning.

WARLORD TRAIT

If a **GENESTEALER CULTS CHARACTER** is your Warlord, you can choose to give them the following Warlord Trait:

FOCUS OF ADORATION

This warlord inspires such insane devotion that his minions will leap into battle in order to win his favour.

Friendly **GENESTEALER CULT INFANTRY** units can perform a Heroic Intervention whilst they are within 6" of this Warlord, even if they are not **CHARACTERS**.

RELIC

If your army is led by a **GENESTEALER CULTS** Warlord, then you may give the following Relic to an Acolyte Iconward in your army.

ICON OF THE CULT ASCENDANT

Cast in blood-blessed platinum, its wyrm-forms polished to a high sheen, the Icon of the Cult Ascendant has been bathed in the psychic energies of the Broodmind. The relic adorned the back of the Great Patriarch's throne for many centuries, soaking up his sheer otherness until it imbued every mote of metal and scrap of oiled cloth. As the time of war comes to pass, the icon is detached from its resting place with the greatest of care and given to the cult's foremost Iconward. Those who fight in its shadow find the power of the Broodmind thrilling through their veins.

Add 1 to the Strength characteristic of friendly **GENESTEALER CULT INFANTRY** units whilst they are within 6" of the bearer.

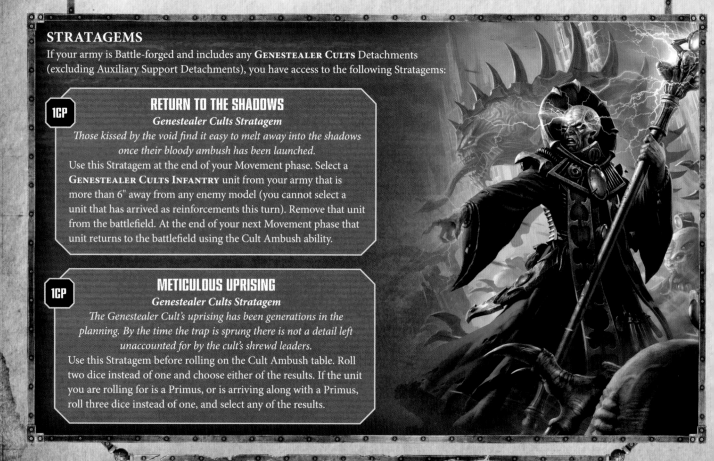

STRATAGEMS

If your army is Battle-forged and includes any **GENESTEALER CULTS** Detachments (excluding Auxiliary Support Detachments), you have access to the following Stratagems:

1CP

RETURN TO THE SHADOWS
Genestealer Cults Stratagem

Those kissed by the void find it easy to melt away into the shadows once their bloody ambush has been launched.

Use this Stratagem at the end of your Movement phase. Select a **GENESTEALER CULTS INFANTRY** unit from your army that is more than 6" away from any enemy model (you cannot select a unit that has arrived as reinforcements this turn). Remove that unit from the battlefield. At the end of your next Movement phase that unit returns to the battlefield using the Cult Ambush ability.

1CP

METICULOUS UPRISING
Genestealer Cults Stratagem

The Genestealer Cult's uprising has been generations in the planning. By the time the trap is sprung there is not a detail left unaccounted for by the cult's shrewd leaders.

Use this Stratagem before rolling on the Cult Ambush table. Roll two dice instead of one and choose either of the results. If the unit you are rolling for is a Primus, or is arriving along with a Primus, roll three dice instead of one, and select any of the results.

HARLEQUINS

For the Harlequins, there is no distinction between art and war, for the warrior-dancers of the Laughing God have always revelled in the dark splendour of battle. They combine psychedelic flair with the pinpoint skill of the master duellist, every slicing shuriken or stabbing blade a stitch in the tapestry of carnage they weave.

Designer's Note: *The following rules cannot be used by any units in a Detachment that contains units with the* **Ynnari** *keyword.*

WARLORD TRAIT

If a **Harlequins Character** (other than a Solitaire) is your Warlord, you can choose to give them the following Warlord Trait:

LUCK OF THE LAUGHING GOD

To be possessed of supernatural fortune is a sure sign of Cegorach's favour.

You can re-roll hit rolls of 1 for this Warlord.

RELIC

If your army is led by a **Harlequins** Warlord, then you may give the following Relic to a **Harlequins Character** in your army.

THE MASK OF SECRETS

Many believe the Mask of Secrets to be no more than a dark fable, yet it is very real, kept within a shadowed vault deep within the Black Library. All who look upon this mask see distorted reflections of their own faults and failings, the slightest doubt or regret twisted into a horrific swarm of phantasms that scream and wail as they claw at the psyche of the victim. Those who wear the Mask of Secrets fear nothing while the mask remains upon their face, yet it is said that in the long run they must pay a terrible price for this temporary boon.

The bearer increases their Leadership characteristic by 1. In addition, all enemy units reduce their Leadership characteristic by 1 whilst they are within 6" of the bearer.

STRATAGEMS

If your army is Battle-forged and includes any **Harlequins** Detachments (excluding Auxiliary Support Detachments), you have access to the following Stratagems:

1CP/3CP

WEBWAY ASSAULT
Harlequins Stratagem

Slipping from the webway with exaggerated stealth, the players of the Harlequins creep behind enemy lines before they attack.
Use this Stratagem during deployment. If you spend 1 CP, you can set up one **Harlequins Infantry** or **Biker** unit from your army in the webway instead of placing it on the battlefield. If you spend 3 CPs, you can set up two such units in the webway instead. Units in the webway can emerge at the end of any of your Movement phases – set them up anywhere on the battlefield that is more than 9" from any enemy units. You can only use this Stratagem once per battle.

1CP

PRISMATIC BLUR
Harlequins Stratagem

A Harlequin's holo-suit projects a shimmering lightstorm of colour as they move; the faster they travel the more pronounced the effect.
Use this Stratagem after a **Harlequins** unit from your army has Advanced; that unit has a 3+ invulnerable save until the start of your next turn.

IMPERIAL KNIGHTS

Imperial Knights are towering war engines, tank-crushing giants that dominate the battlefield. These powerful bipedal suits bear massive weapons capable of unleashing immense destruction. A single Knight is more than a match for a tank squadron, while an entire formation wields enough power to level a hive city. To witness an army of these titanic machines is to see first-hand the glorious might of the Imperium.

Designer's Note: *If your army is Battle-forged and includes a* **Questor Imperialis** *or* **Questor Mechanicus** *Super-Heavy Detachment – that is, a Super-Heavy Detachment where every unit has the* **Questor Imperialis** *keyword or every unit has the* **Questor Mechanicus** *keyword, one model in that Detachment can gain the* **Character** *keyword, and so can be your Warlord and be equipped with a Relic.*

WARLORD TRAIT

If a **Questor Imperialis Character** or a **Questor Mechanicus Character** is your Warlord, you can choose to give them the following Warlord Trait:

Knight Seneschal

Veteran warriors who have proved themselves worthy time and again in the fires of battle are awarded the rank of Knight Seneschal.

Add 1 to this Warlord's Attacks characteristic.

RELIC

If your army is led by a **Questor Imperialis** or **Questor Mechanicus** Warlord, then you may give the following Relic to a **Questor Imperialis** or **Questor Mechanicus** (as appropriate) **Character** in your army.

Ravager

This storied reaper chainblade has claimed millions of lives during its long service to the knightly houses. The chainblade's razor-sharp teeth were harvested from the canines of a long-extinct species of bio-horror called a Balethrox. What makes this fact so startling is that dozens of the fell creatures must have been hunted down and slain by brave Knights in order to secure enough fangs to line Ravager's cutting blade. However, witnessing the murderous wrath of this chainblade's touch in battle more than justifies the dedication of those long-dead Knights, and its bearer will fight all the harder to honour their sacrifice.

Model with a reaper chainsword only. Ravager replaces the bearer's reaper chainsword and has the following profile:

WEAPON	RANGE	TYPE	S	AP	D
Ravager	Melee	Melee	+6	-3	6
Abilities: You can re-roll hit rolls of 1 for this weapon.					

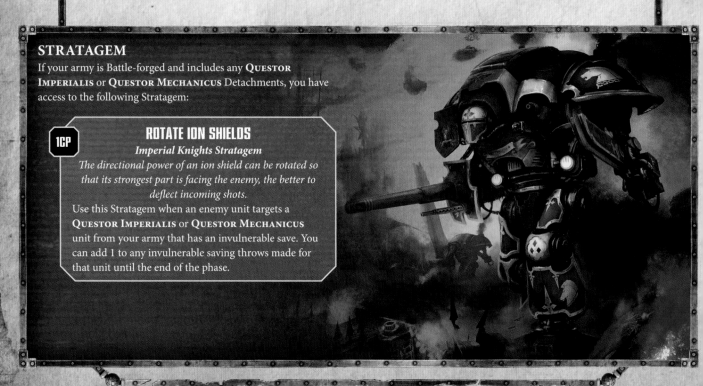

STRATAGEM

If your army is Battle-forged and includes any **Questor Imperialis** or **Questor Mechanicus** Detachments, you have access to the following Stratagem:

1CP

ROTATE ION SHIELDS
Imperial Knights Stratagem
The directional power of an ion shield can be rotated so that its strongest part is facing the enemy, the better to deflect incoming shots.
Use this Stratagem when an enemy unit targets a **Questor Imperialis** or **Questor Mechanicus** unit from your army that has an invulnerable save. You can add 1 to any invulnerable saving throws made for that unit until the end of the phase.

NECRONS

Deep within the darkness of the void, ancient tomb worlds stir once more to life as the Necron race claws its way towards the stars. Aeons ago, they ruled vast swathes of the galaxy as cruel immortal masters, their people having forsaken frail mortal flesh for deathless living-metal bodies. For millennia they slumbered, awaiting an age when the galaxy would be ripe for conquest. That time is now. The Necrons are awakening in their billions, their vast armies led by tyrants hungry to reclaim their empire of old.

WARLORD TRAIT

If a **Necron Character** (other than a **C'tan Shard**) is your Warlord, you can choose to give them the following Warlord Trait:

Enduring Will

This Warlord is possessed of iron resolve and no mortal weaponry will prevent him from achieving his goals.

Reduce any damage inflicted on your Warlord by 1 (to a minimum of 1). For example, if your Warlord fails a saving throw against a weapon that inflicts 3 damage, they will only lose 2 wounds.

RELIC

If your army is led by a **Necron** Warlord, then you may give the following Relic to a **Necron Character** (other than a **C'tan Shard**) in your army.

The Veil of Darkness

This device was fashioned from transpositanium, a substance so rare that it can only be found in a handful of places in the galaxy. It is highly sought after by the Necrons, and wars have been waged to secure it. Activated with a thought, the veil causes space and time to warp around its user and those near them, enfolding them in a swirling darkness. As the darkness fades, the user and their comrades appear elsewhere on the battlefield, transported through a miracle of arcane science.

Once per battle, at the end of any of your Movement phases, the bearer can use the Veil of Darkness. When they do, the bearer, and up to one friendly <Dynasty> Infantry unit within 3" of the bearer, are removed from the battlefield. Then, set up the bearer (and the second unit you chose, if any) anywhere on the battlefield that is more than 9" from any enemy models (the second unit must be set up wholly within 6" of the bearer).

STRATAGEMS

If your army is Battle-forged and includes any **Necrons** Detachments (excluding Auxiliary Support Detachments), you have access to the following Stratagems:

2CP

REPAIR SUBROUTINES
Necrons Stratagem
When engaged in a battle of attrition, Canoptek constructs react by enabling a series of adaptive subroutines, allowing them to better focus on self-repair.
Use this Stratagem at the start of your turn, before making any Reanimation Protocols rolls. Select a **Canoptek** unit from your army that is on the battlefield. That unit gains the Reanimation Protocols ability until the end of your turn.

2CP

ENHANCED REANIMATION PROTOCOLS
Necrons Stratagem
The Necrons are a deathless foe that can recover from obliteration time and again.
Use this Stratagem before making Reanimation Protocols rolls for a unit from your army. You can re-roll Reanimation Protocols rolls of 1 for that unit this turn.

ORKS

Orks fall upon their foes like an avalanche, a vast horde of barbaric green-skinned warriors wielding an assortment of crude but deadly weapons. Resilient, resourceful and incredibly numerous, their race's murderous rampages are a deadly threat to the galaxy. They are addicted to the sound of gunfire, to speeding about in ramshackle vehicles, and to violence and brutality in all its forms.

WARLORD TRAIT

If an **ORK CHARACTER** is your Warlord, you can choose to give them the following Warlord Trait:

MIGHT IS RIGHT

Made of muscle and aggression, this Warlord is the embodiment of the Orks' warlike nature.

Add 1 to this Warlord's Strength characteristic.

RELIC

If your army is led by an **ORK** Warlord, then you may give the following Relic to an **ORK CHARACTER** in your army.

HEADWOPPA'S KILLCHOPPA

Grand Warboss Headwoppa had a real thing for decapitating his enemies. Whenever the Warboss lopped the head from an opponent, his ladz would raise a raucous cheer. Headwoppa and his tribe were last seen charging headlong into a horde of Khornate Daemons, but legend speaks of a blood-slick big choppa that still turns up occasionally. Though this weapon looks normal, a dark voice is said to growl into the mind of its wielder, driving them on to ever greater excesses of violence.

Model with a big choppa only. Headwoppa's Killchoppa replaces the bearer's big choppa and has the following profile:

WEAPON	RANGE	TYPE	S	AP	D
Headwoppa's Killchoppa	Melee	Melee	+2	-2	D3
Abilities: Wound rolls of 6+ made for this weapon inflict D3 mortal wounds instead of the normal damage.					

STRATAGEMS

If your army is Battle-forged and includes any **ORK** Detachments (excluding Auxiliary Support Detachments), you have access to the following Stratagems:

1CP

MOB UP
Orks Stratagem

Smaller Ork mobs tend to be caught up and swept along when a large enough horde of greenskins stampedes across the battlefield.

Use this Stratagem at the end of your Movement phase. Select two **ORK INFANTRY** units from your army that are within 2" of each other that have the same datasheet (e.g. choose two Boyz units, or two Stormboyz units). If one of the units has 10 or more models, and the other has 10 or fewer, the two units merge and, for the rest of the battle, they are counted as a single unit for all rules purposes.

1CP

DAKKA! DAKKA! DAKKA!
Orks Stratagem

There is no such thing as too much dakka.

Use this Stratagem before an **ORK INFANTRY** or **BIKER** unit from your army shoots in your Shooting phase. Each time you make a hit roll of 6+ for a model in that unit, immediately make an extra attack against the same unit using the same weapon. These extra attacks cannot themselves generate any further attacks.

SPACE WOLVES

The Sons of Russ are a proud brethren, as noble as they are fierce. Riding to battle in the company of monstrous wolves, growling war machines and living legends whose sagas span millennia, these Space Marines may appear to be wild, perhaps even barbaric. Yet their loyalty to the Imperium has been proven beyond doubt. They are the Space Wolves, and in them, the fury of storm-wracked Fenris has been tempered by the cold cunning of the hunt. Woe betide those they mark as their prey, for they too shall feel the fangs of the wolf around their throats…

WARLORD TRAIT

If a **Space Wolves Character** is your Warlord, you can give them the following Warlord Trait:

Saga of the Warrior Born

Endowed with preternatural prowess, the warlord strikes swift and savage at all who stand before him.

You can always choose your Warlord to fight first in the Fight phase even if he didn't charge. If the enemy has units that have charged, or that have a similar ability, then alternate choosing units to fight with, starting with the player whose turn is taking place.

RELIC

If your army is led by a **Space Wolves** Warlord, then you may give the following Relic to a **Space Wolves Character** in your army.

Krakenbone Sword

The Krakenbone Sword was carved from the sternum of a gigantic ocean beast by a smith of the Iron Blood tribe and presented to a young Logan Grimnar. Though it has remained ever sharp, Arjac Rockfist reworked the blade, making it even more deadly, and it is now one of Fenris' most prized heirlooms.

Model with frost sword only. The Krakenbone Sword replaces the bearer's frost sword and has the following profile:

WEAPON	RANGE	TYPE	S	AP	D
Krakenbone Sword	Melee	Melee	+1	-4	1
Abilities: You can re-roll failed wound rolls for this weapon.					

STRATAGEM

If your army is Battle-forged and includes any **Space Wolves** Detachments (excluding Auxiliary Support Detachments), you have access to the following Stratagems:

1CP
TRUE GRIT
Space Wolves Stratagem
The Sons of Russ drill for extreme close-quarters firefights. Use this Stratagem in your Shooting phase. Choose a **Space Wolves Infantry** unit from your army that is within 1" of an enemy unit. In this phase, models in that unit can fire their auto bolt rifles, boltguns, bolt rifles and bolt carbines as if they had the Pistol 2 Type. Models that do so cannot fire any other Pistols in this phase.

1CP
CUNNING OF THE WOLF
Space Wolves Stratagem
The most successful hunts are those where the prey doesn't know they are being hunted.
Use this Stratagem during deployment, when setting up a **Space Wolves Infantry** unit. You can set up this unit on the hunt instead of placing it on the battlefield. At the end of any of your Movement phases the unit can join the battle – set it up so that it is wholly within 6" of any battlefield edge of your choice and more than 9" away from any enemy models.

T'AU EMPIRE

A dynamic race whose technology eclipses anything their foes can muster, the T'au use speed, resilience and overwhelming firepower to win their battles. Guided by the mysterious Ethereal caste, all T'au strive for the Greater Good of their empire, forging ever onward into the stars to bring enlightenment at the barrel of a gun.

WARLORD TRAIT

If a **T'AU EMPIRE CHARACTER** is your Warlord, you can choose to give them one of the two Warlord Traits described below. Alternatively, you can roll a D6 to randomly select one of them; on a 1-3 your Warlord has the Exemplar of the Kauyon trait, and on a 4-6 they have the Exemplar of the Mont'ka trait.

EXEMPLAR OF THE KAUYON

This Warlord has studied every aspect of the Patient Hunter strategy; there are no finer proponents of its use in the T'au Empire.

You can re-roll failed hit rolls for your Warlord as long as they have not moved this turn. If they have moved for any reason, they lose this trait until the start of their next turn.

EXEMPLAR OF THE MONT'KA

This Warlord has honed the art of the Killing Blow to a fine art, as has been proven on a hundred battlefields.

This Warlord can Advance and still shoot as if they hadn't moved this turn.

RELIC

If your army is led by a **T'AU EMPIRE** Warlord, then you may give the following Relic to a **T'AU EMPIRE CHARACTER** in your army.

PURETIDE ENGRAM NEUROCHIP

Commander Puretide was undoubtedly the most gifted T'au Commander of all time. The T'au were unwilling to lose his tactical and strategic brilliance, and upon his death, his mind was scanned and his accumulated memories committed to a massive hologram on his birth world of Dal'yth. A sliver of that genius has been crafted into a bio-chip. When surgically implanted into the brain of a Fire caste commander, the bearer can access much of the wisdom and tactical acumen of Puretide himself.

Once per battle, you can re-roll a single hit roll, wound roll or damage roll made for the bearer, or a friendly <Sept> unit within 6" of the bearer. In addition, if your army is Battle-forged and the bearer is on the battlefield, roll a D6 each time you or your opponent use a Stratagem; on a 6 you gain a bonus Command Point.

STRATAGEM

If your army is Battle-forged and includes any **T'AU EMPIRE** Detachments (excluding Auxiliary Support Detachments), you have access to the following Stratagem:

1CP — **UPLINKED MARKERLIGHT**
T'au Empire Stratagem
Some markerlights are uplinked directly into the T'au command network, enabling a much faster and more accurate degree of tactical targeting support.
Use this Stratagem after an enemy unit has been hit by a markerlight fired by a model from your army. Place D3+1 markerlight counters next to that unit instead of only 1.

THOUSAND SONS

The Thousand Sons are a Traitor Legion of power-armoured automata. Relentless, fearless and formidably resilient, the Thousand Sons advance inexorably upon their foes and blast them apart with volleys of warp-tainted firepower. They are guided into battle by powerful Sorcerers who expend their warriors like pawns, while flaying the enemy with the unbridled energies of change.

WARLORD TRAIT

If a **THOUSAND SONS CHARACTER** is your Warlord, you can give them the following Warlord Trait:

ARROGANCE OF AEONS

This Warlord draws strength from a long-harboured hubris; the idea of submitting to the arcane will of another is anathema to him.

Re-roll failed Deny the Witch tests you take for this Warlord.

RELIC

If your army is led by a **THOUSAND SONS** Warlord, then you may give the following Relic to a **THOUSAND SONS PSYKER CHARACTER** in your army.

ATHENAEAN SCROLLS

The arch-sorcerer Ahriman consumed the knowledge contained in the Athenaeum of Kallimakus long ago. However, not all of the Athenaeum's founders were slain when their repository of knowledge was destroyed. Some of their Apollonian disciplines have since been transcribed on sanctified papyrus in order to keep an echo of that great library in existence. One who possesses the so-called 'Athenaean Scrolls' has access to advanced psychic techniques that make their spells all but unstoppable.

If you roll a double when making a successful Psychic test for the bearer, your opponent cannot attempt to resist that psychic power with a Deny the Witch test or negate it by any means. Note that the psyker will still suffer Perils of the Warp on a roll of double 1 or double 6, and if slain by Perils of the Warp, the power they were trying to manifest will still automatically fail.

PSYCHIC POWERS

Before the battle, a **THOUSAND SONS PSYKER** can replace a psychic power (not *Smite*) with the following:

TZEENTCH'S FIRESTORM

The psyker conjures a storm of multi-hued fire that mutates his enemy's flesh and burns their souls.

Tzeentch's Firestorm has a warp charge value of 7. If manifested, select an enemy unit that is within 18" of the psyker and visible to him. Roll 9 dice; the enemy unit you selected suffers a mortal wound for each roll of a 6.

STRATAGEM

If your army is Battle-forged and includes any **THOUSAND SONS** Detachments (excluding Auxiliary Support Detachments), you have access to the following Stratagem:

1CP

CABALISTIC FOCUS
Thousand Sons Stratagem

When the sorcerers of the Thousand Sons combine their arcane powers, they unleash terrible and unstoppable magic.

Use this Stratagem before attempting to manifest a psychic power with a **THOUSAND SONS PSYKER** from your army that is within 6" of at least 2 other friendly **THOUSAND SONS PSYKERS**. You can add 2 to the Psychic test.

APPENDIX

In this section you will find a collection of supplementary content that you can use in any of your games of Warhammer 40,000.

Battlefield Terrain

This section provides rules for a range of terrain pieces that can be used to transform your gaming table into an interactive, thematic battlefield.

With the Deathworld Forest terrain, you can add sprawling thickets of lethal plant life to your games, forcing warriors to battle their way through grasping tendrils and weather salvoes of toxic spines as they do battle with one another.

Alternatively, using the Hive City terrain rules, you can lace your battlefields with thrumming wonders of arcane technology. Siphon searing plasma from conduits to supercharge your weaponry, or blast apart shuddering generators in order to annihilate the foes cowering in their shadows. Such exciting terrain can add a whole new dimension to your games of Warhammer 40,000.

Battlezones

Here you will find rules for two Battlezones that expand on the rules in the *Warhammer 40,000* rulebook.

The first of these allows you to fight running battles through the tangled sprawl of industrial worlds. From scaling the flanks of chugging manufactorum machinery using grappling lines, to raining explosives down on your foes from high gantries or unleashing blazing promethium, this section provides a set of Stratagems for use in such industrialised war zones.

The second set of Battlezone rules depicts the horror of fighting amidst the madness of an empyric storm. Including a range of events that represent the insane warping of reality, these Battlezone rules bring an exciting element of unpredictability to your battles.

'SURVIVAL IS NO BIRTHRIGHT, BUT A PRIZE WRESTED FROM AN UNCARING GALAXY BY FORGOTTEN HEROES.'

- *Tactica Imperium*

Ladder Campaigns

One of the most enjoyable aspects of the Warhammer 40,000 hobby is playing campaigns. Linking multiple games together into a single, ongoing contest, players find the stakes of every conflict increasing as they compete to see who can rise to primacy and claim victory in the campaign as a whole.

Ladder campaigns are one of the simplest and most straightforward examples of this sort of gaming. This section explains how to organise one, how to keep it running and how to determine who will eventually claim victory and prove themselves the mightiest tabletop commander.

Updated Points Values

The points values we give to each unit allow players to organise their armies based on the strength of each element, and are a great tool when collecting a force for the tabletop.

With each new publication, we review the points values we have given to each unit, and update them if necessary. Here you will find lists of all the updated points values for such units, including several from the Forge World range.

Battle-forged Armies

In this final section of the Appendix, you will find useful tools to help you keep track of the details of your Battle-forged armies.

Once you have a suitably impressive collection of Citadel Miniatures, it is always satisfying to add up their points as an army, either simply to figure out how much your army is worth, or to fine-tune it to a specific points value ready to play games with other hobbyists.

However, while many people enjoy the process of adding up their army's points and designing the perfect army list to take to battle, it helps to be able to keep track of that information so that all you need to do each time you start a game is crack open your case, place your models on the table, and get playing.

The Detachment and army rosters at the end of the Appendix allow you to do just this, with space to record details of each of your units – including their wargear options, Battlefield Role and points values – as well as each Detachment in your army, for easy reference as you play your games of Warhammer 40,000.

BATTLEFIELD TERRAIN

Here we present rules for some of the environmental challenges faced by those deployed for battle on distant planets, from lethal plants to hazardous industrial complexes. These are new additions to the expanded rules for battlefield terrain that can be found in the *Warhammer 40,000* rulebook.

DEATHWORLD FORESTS

Razor-sharp walls of crystalline growths, remnants of ancient civilisations long since overgrown and sentient flora that ensnare and consume the unwary are but a few of the dangers that can be found lurking in the perilous alien forests of the galaxy.

A Deathworld Forest consists of one or more of the following terrain pieces in any combination: Shardwrack Spines, Eldritch Ruins, Barbed Venomgorse or Grapple Weeds. Each piece of Deathworld Forest terrain is a separate model.

When a model targets an enemy **Infantry** unit that has all of its models within 1" of a Deathworld Forest terrain piece, the target unit receives the benefit of cover if the attacking model is closer to the terrain piece than it is to the target. In addition, subtract 1 from hit rolls for models that make close combat attacks within 3" of a Deathworld Forest terrain piece – this represents limbs being entangled by sentient roots or minds being fogged by eldritch energies.

Each of the four Deathworld Forest terrain pieces has an additional ability, as described opposite.

ELDRITCH RUIN

An aura of arcane power surrounds these ancient ruins.

You can add 1 to Psychic tests and Deny the Witch tests you make for **PSYKERS** that are within 3" of any Eldritch Ruin terrain pieces.

GRAPPLE WEED

These lethal plants uproot themselves to seek out their prey.

Roll a D6 each time a model moves within 3" of a Grapple Weed terrain piece whilst Advancing or charging – on a roll of 1, that model's unit suffers D3 mortal wounds. In addition, at the start of each battle round, each Grapple Weed terrain piece moves 2D6" in a straight line towards the nearest visible unit, provided there are any within 12". If two or more units are equidistant, roll off to see which one it moves towards. When moving a Grapple Weed terrain piece, it will stop 1" away from any units or any other battlefield terrain. After it has moved, roll a D6 for each unit within 3" of any Grapple Weed terrain pieces. On a 4+, that unit suffers a mortal wound.

SHARDWRACK SPINE

This deadly flora shoots piercing spines at its prey.

Roll a D6 each time a model moves within 6" of a Shardwrack Spine terrain pieces whilst Advancing or charging – on a roll of 1, the model's unit suffers a mortal wound.

BARBED VENOMGORSE

The throttling limbs of barbed venomgorse are swift and strong.

Roll a D6 each time a model moves within 3" of a Barbed Venomgorse terrain piece whilst Advancing or charging – on a roll of 1 or 2, that model's unit suffers a mortal wound.

SECTOR MECHANICUS

Sectors Mechanicus are a common sight throughout the galaxy, utilitarian structures of gantries and girders that thrum with automated industry, belching black smoke as they feed the Imperium's ravenous hunger for war materiel.

Unless they can **FLY**, **VEHICLES**, **MONSTERS**, **CAVALRY** and **BIKERS** can only be set up and end their moves on the ground floor of a Sector Mechanicus structure. Unless they can **FLY**, **INFANTRY** and **BEASTS** must scale ladders, girders or walls to ascend or descend between the different levels of a Sector Mechanicus structure. **INFANTRY** are also assumed to be able to traverse around girders, buttresses and hanging chains, and so move through them without impediment.

INFANTRY units that are on a Sector Mechanicus structure receive the benefit of cover. Other units only receive the benefit of cover if at least 50% of every model is obscured from the point of view of the shooting unit.

HAEMOTROPE REACTOR

These store vast amounts of power, making them objects of cover for the brave only.

Units within 3" of a Haemotrope Reactor that are at least 25% obscured by it, from the point of view of the firing unit, receive the benefit of cover.

Roll a D6 each time you make a saving throw of 7+ (such as a roll of 6, plus 1 for being in cover) for a model within 3" of any Haemotrope Reactors in the Shooting phase. On a 1, the model's unit suffers a mortal wound.

THERMIC PLASMA REGULATORS

These ancient machines thrum with lethal plasma energy.

Thermic Plasma Regulators follow all the rules for Sector Mechanicus structures with the following addition:

Roll a D6 each time you make a saving throw of 7+ (such as a roll of 6, plus 1 for being in cover) for a model within 3" of any Thermic Plasma Regulators in the Shooting phase. On a 1, the model's unit suffers a mortal wound.

THERMIC PLASMA CONDUITS

These conduits channel hot plasma and make for dangerous cover.

When a model targets an enemy **INFANTRY** unit that has all of its models within 1" of a Thermic Plasma Conduit, the target unit receives the benefit of cover if the attacking model is closer to the Thermic Plasma Conduit than it is to the target. In addition, enemy units can Fight across a Thermic Plasma Conduit, even if the physical distance is more than 1". When resolving Fights between units on opposite sides of a Thermic Plasma Conduit, units can be chosen to Fight and can make their attacks if the enemy is within 2", instead of 1".

Roll a D6 each time you make a saving throw of 7+ (such as a roll of 6, plus 1 for being in cover) for a model within 1" of any Thermic Plasma Conduits in the Shooting phase. On a 1, the model's unit suffers a mortal wound.

BATTLEZONE: INDUSTRIAL WORLDS

So long as you and your opponent agree, any Warhammer 40,000 battle can use Battlezone rules. If you choose these Battlezone rules, your forces can interact with the Sector Mechanicus structures upon which they fight. They can pour fire down on their foes from their elevated positions or tap into plasma feeds and promethium lines to increase their weapons' destructive potential.

Height Advantage: A model gains a Height Advantage whilst occupying the upper levels of a Sector Mechanicus structure and shooting at a unit that is at a lower level. To gain a Height Advantage, every model in the target unit must be 3" or more below the firing model. If a model shoots with a Height Advantage, the target does not receive bonuses to their saving throws for being in cover.

STRATAGEMS

In this battlezone, you and your opponent can both use Command Points (CPs) to use any of the following Stratagems:

1CP
GRAPPLING HOOKS
Industrial Worlds Stratagem
A crude but effective means of claiming the high ground.
Use this Stratagem at the start of your Movement phase. Select one of your **INFANTRY** units. For the duration of your turn, models in this unit can ascend or descend Sector Mechanicus structures when they move, even without a ladder, wall or girder. Furthermore, for the duration of your turn, do not count any vertical distance that unit moves against the total they can move that turn (i.e. moving vertically is free for those models).

2CP
POWER SUPPLY
Industrial Worlds Stratagem
The molten blood of the Omnissiah flows ever onward.
Use this Stratagem at the start of any turn. Select a Void Shield Generator that is within 6" of a Haemotrope Reactor, or that is connected to a Haemotrope Reactor or a Thermic Plasma Regulator by either Fuel Pipes or Thermic Plasma Conduits. The invulnerable save afforded by the Void Shield Generator is 4+ until the end of the turn.

1CP
OVERLOAD POWER CORE
Industrial Worlds Stratagem
Crudely desecrated, this volatile device makes a potent bomb.
Use this Stratagem before an **INFANTRY** model from your army that is within 1" of a Plasma Conduit throws a grenade. Instead of a grenade, that model hurls a power core at the foe. You only make a single hit roll, but if you hit the target it suffers D3 mortal wounds.

1CP
PLASMA FEED
Industrial Worlds Stratagem
The Omnissiah's grace can be siphoned and turned upon the foe.
Select an **INFANTRY** unit from your army that is within 1" of any Thermic Plasma Regulators or Conduits before it shoots in the Shooting phase, or before it fires Overwatch. Until the end of this phase, add 1 to the Strength and Damage characteristics of all plasma weapons the unit is equipped with. For the purposes of this Stratagem, a plasma weapon is any weapon profile whose name includes the word 'plasma' (e.g. plasma pistol, plasma gun, plasma rifle, plasma incinerator).

1CP
SIPHON PROMETHIUM
Industrial Worlds Stratagem
A quick and risky transfusion of refined promethium makes flamer weapons all the more lethal.
Select an **INFANTRY** unit from your army that is within 1" of any Fuel Pipes before it shoots in the Shooting phase, or before it fires Overwatch. Until the end of this phase, double the range of all flame weapons the squad is equipped with and add 1 to any wound rolls made for these weapons. For the purposes of this Stratagem, a flame weapon is an Ork burna, skorcha or any weapon profile whose name includes the word 'flame' (e.g. flamer, heavy flamer, flamestorm gauntlet).

1CP
SUPERCHARGED OBLITERATION
Industrial Worlds Stratagem
Power surges down blessed conduits, allowing the Omnissiah's wrath to surge forth again and again.
Use this Stratagem after you have fired a Plasma Obliterator in the Shooting phase. If that building is within 6" of a Haemotrope Reactor, fire the Plasma Obliterator again.

1CP
LONG BOMB
Industrial Worlds Stratagem
Munitions hurled from on high rain down with great fury.
Use this Stratagem before a unit from your army shoots in the Shooting phase. If a model in that unit has a Height Advantage, you can double the range of any Grenade weapons it uses this phase.

BATTLEZONE: EMPYRIC STORMS

So long as you and your opponent agree, any Warhammer 40,000 battle can use Battlezone rules. If you have chosen these Battlezone rules, raging warp tides will affect your armies and their surroundings, changing the laws of reality, manifesting fell creatures and imbuing psykers with unfathomable power.

Raging Storms: Each player must generate a single Empyric Storms event at the start of each of their turns. To generate an Empyric Storms event, roll two dice, one after the other: the first dice represents tens and the second represents digits, giving you a result between 11 and 66. Then consult the table on the right.

Some Empyric Storms events are 'Instantaneous' – these are resolved as soon as they are generated. Other events are 'Persistent'. If you generate a Persistent event, the effects listed for that event apply to both players until the start of your next turn, at which point they will cease to have any effect and you will then generate a new event. If a Persistent event that is already in effect is generated, then a new event should be generated instead.

Empyric Reinforcements

Some Empyric Storm events can summon a new unit to the battlefield, or transform one model into a different model. Note that these new units do not cost either player any points in a matched play game. They cannot include any additional models, but can otherwise be given any upgrades or options normally available to them. The event that creates a new unit will describe how to set it up on the battlefield. It cannot move in the Movement phase of the turn in which it is set up, and counts as having moved for any rules purposes (e.g. if firing Heavy weapons, etc.), but can otherwise act normally during the rest of its turn (i.e. it can shoot, charge, etc.).

BATTLEZONE: EMPYRIC STORMS CARD DECK

If you own a deck of Battlezone: Empyric Storms cards, you can generate your Empyric Storms event by shuffling the deck and drawing the top card instead of rolling a D66. These should be kept face up so that you and your opponent can both see what events are currently in play.

EMPYRIC STORMS TABLE

D66	RESULT	TYPE
11	Psychic Interference	Persistent
12	Psychic Boon	Persistent
13	Empyric Shield	Persistent
14	Null Tide	Persistent
15	Total Power	Persistent
16	The Denizens Hunger	Persistent
21	Warp Surge	Persistent
22	Warp Ebb	Persistent
23	Psychic Apotheosis	Instantaneous
24	Warp Tunnel	Instantaneous
25	Reality Speeds	Persistent
26	Reality Slows	Persistent
31	Warp Shadows	Persistent
32	Empyric Might	Persistent
33	Empyric Resilience	Persistent
34	Empyric Fury	Persistent
35	Empyric Courage	Persistent
36	Empyric Terror	Persistent
41	Warp Regeneration	Instantaneous
42	Empyric Foresight	Persistent
43	Empyric Feedback	Instantaneous
44	Conduit of the Immaterium	Instantaneous
45	Warp Resurrection	Instantaneous
46	Empyric Mastery	Persistent
51	Overwhelming Power	Persistent
52	The Warp Becalmed	Persistent
53	Psychic Devastation	Persistent
54	Empyric Invulnerability	Persistent
55	Uncontrolled Mutation	Instantaneous
56	Dark Possession	Instantaneous
61	Terrors of the Warp	Persistent
62	Warp Blast	Instantaneous
63	Unreality Reigns	Persistent
64	Psychic Stun	Instantaneous
65	Daemontide	Instantaneous
66	Empyric Breach	Instantaneous

11 — PSYCHIC INTERFERENCE — *Persistent*

Screaming voices clamour upon the winds of the Empyrean. Surging psychic static fills the thoughts of psykers across the battlefield, fouling their connection to the powers of the warp and making it ever more difficult to focus. Powers sputter and fizzle, dispersing like mist amidst a gale.

Increase the warp charge value of all psychic powers by 1.

12 — PSYCHIC BOON — *Persistent*

Wave upon wave of warp energy flows across the battlefield, like an incoming tide that inundates a drowning shore. Eyes burning with power, the psykers of the warring armies find themselves able to siphon off all the empyric energies they require to fuel even their most terrifying abilities.

Decrease the warp charge cost of all psychic powers by 1 (to a minimum of 1).

13 — EMPYRIC SHIELD — *Persistent*

Billowing soul-mists roll in across the battlefield, barely perceptible yet cloying and thick. They gather about warriors fighting all across the battlefield, shifting in and out of reality at random. Where the warp mists solidify, blasts and blades are stopped dead.

All models gain a 6+ invulnerable save. If a model already has an invulnerable save, you can instead add 1 to the roll when making invulnerable saving throws for it.

14 — NULL TIDE — *Persistent*

Entropic currents drag at the warring armies, moaning data ghosts and rip-tides of misery draining away the protective powers of sorcery and technology alike. Power fields flicker out in showers of sparks. Sorcerous barriers fade like smoke. Even Daemons find themselves stripped of their normal empyric defences by the sucking null tide.

Models cannot use invulnerable saves.

15 — TOTAL POWER — *Persistent*

A raging squall of fury sweeps across the battlefield, downpours of glowing crimson ectoplasm splattering upon every surface. Searing rage fills the minds of the battling psykers, charging them with energy and transforming their powers into empyric battering rams.

If a **PSYKER** rolls any doubles when taking a Psychic test, that power is automatically manifested and no attempts to Deny the Witch can be made to resist it.

16 — THE DENIZENS HUNGER — *Persistent*

As the veil of reality thins, so terrible warp predators begin to circle like sharks drawn by blood in the ocean. Across the battlefield, psykers shudder and struggle to focus as they feel questing tendrils brush their minds, and hot, sulphurous breath upon the backs of their necks.

If a **PSYKER** rolls any doubles when taking a Psychic test, they suffer Perils of the Warp.

21 — WARP SURGE — *Persistent*

As howling psychic gales blast across the battlefield, warring psykers find the distance across which they can hurl their powers greatly magnified. Sorcerous flames and psychic shields alike are carried far and fast upon the surging tides of the empyrean.

The range of all psychic powers is doubled.

22 — WARP EBB — *Persistent*

Though warp storms rage beyond the veil, this battlefield has become becalmed. The powers of the immaterium fade, until it becomes difficult for psykers to project their powers even beyond the cages of their own minds. For some warriors this proves a reprieve, for others it is a curse.

The range of all psychic powers is halved.

23 — PSYCHIC APOTHEOSIS — *Instantaneous*

Boundless change roils beneath the thin skin of reality. Strands of fate are rewoven, and hidden potential is suddenly unlocked. Like dawn breaking through the darkness, a powerful mind is awoken like never before, and a newfound – if dangerous – power is harnessed.

Randomly select one **CHARACTER** in your army that is not a **PSYKER**: that model immediately becomes a **PSYKER** and remains one for the rest of the battle. This model can attempt to manifest the *Smite* psychic power once in each of your Psychic phases. However, this model suffers Perils of the Warp any time they fail a Psychic test.

24 | WARP TUNNEL | *Instantaneous*

As the warp rages, its wayward currents draw in the unwitting and propel them through reality to unexpected quarters. So swift is this transition that those warriors barely have time to realise that they have moved at all.

Select any unit from your army (but not a **Vehicle**) that is more than 1" from any enemy models and remove it from the battlefield. Then, set up that unit anywhere on the battlefield that is more than 9" from any enemy model. The unit cannot move again during the Movement phase of this turn, and counts as having moved for any rules purposes (e.g. if firing Heavy weapons, etc.), but can otherwise act normally during the rest of its turn (i.e. it can shoot, charge, etc.).

25 | REALITY SPEEDS | *Persistent*

Within the aegis of some warp storms, the temporal flow of reality accelerates like water rushing through rocky rapids. Warriors find themselves flung across the battlefield, with those whose souls are bound closest to the warp able to travel swiftest of all.

All models add 1" to their Move characteristic. **Psykers** and **Daemons** add 3" to their Move characteristic instead.

26 | REALITY SLOWS | *Persistent*

The air itself thickens, becoming a leaden, sucking miasma that clings to combatants and slows their advance. Those through whom the warp's energies flow strongest are the worst encumbered, moving as though encased in slowly setting ferrocrete.

All models subtract 1" from their Move characteristic (to a minimum of 0"). **Psykers** and **Daemons** subtract 3" from their Move characteristic instead (to a minimum of 0"). If a model has a minimum and maximum Move characteristic, subtract 1" from the maximum value only.

31 | WARP SHADOWS | *Persistent*

The warp storm brings an unnatural dusk, shrouding the battlefield in shifting shadows and crawling gloom. Warriors peer through the cold darkness, their souls filled with dread at this unnatural phenomenon and the invisible dangers that doubtless lurk within it.

When making hit rolls in the Shooting phase, subtract 1 from the result if the target is more than 12" away from the firing model, subtract 2 if it is more than 24" away, or subtract 3 if it is more than 36" away.

32 | EMPYRIC MIGHT | *Persistent*

Amidst the churning tides of the warp, fanged maws yawn wide to vomit forth the souls of mighty warriors. These soul-echoes bind themselves to the corporeal forms of battling warriors and potent psykers, and lend ethereal might to their blows.

All models add 1 to their Strength characteristic. **Psykers** and **Daemons** add 2 to their Strength characteristic instead.

33 | EMPYRIC RESILIENCE | *Persistent*

A roaring tornado of empyric energy churns across the battlefield. Where it passes over the warring armies, combatants find their flesh toughening like leather, their sinews thickening and skin growing unnatural scales or horned plates that repel attacks from the foe.

All models add 1 to their Toughness characteristic. **Psykers** and **Daemons** add 2 to their Toughness characteristic instead.

34 | EMPYRIC FURY | *Persistent*

Blood-red clouds drift silently down upon the battlefield, settling in a noxious miasma over the warring armies. Warriors find their hearts thudding faster and adrenaline surging as unnatural fury fills them, driving them on to hack and batter madly at their enemies with howls of rage.

All models add 1 to their Attacks characteristic. **Psykers** and **Daemons** add 2 to their Attacks characteristic instead.

35 | EMPYRIC COURAGE | *Persistent*

Singing warp-winds sweep across the battlefield, bringing with them the voices of the heroic dead. Words of encouragement and strength fill the minds of the battling armies, the stirring exhortations of champions long dead steeling their nerves and hardening their hearts.

All models add 1 to their Leadership characteristic. **Psykers** and **Daemons** add 2 to their Leadership characteristic instead.

36 | EMPYRIC TERROR | *Persistent*

As the warp presses close to the skin of reality, malefic spirits seep through to haunt the denizens of realspace. Things shudder and twitch in warriors' peripheral vision. Crawling horror and unreasoning terror fill men's minds, along with the sense that terrible, hateful things lurk just beyond sight.

All models subtract 1 from their Leadership characteristic. **Psykers** and **Daemons** subtract 2 from their Leadership instead.

41 WARP REGENERATION — *Instantaneous*

A rolling storm-surge of empyric energy sweeps across the battlefield, reknitting sundered flesh and setting shattered bone. What the warp takes in exchange for this apparent miracle, none can say, but though seemingly benevolent, there is always a price for such largesse.

Every model on the battlefield regains 1 lost wound.

42 EMPYRIC FORESIGHT — *Persistent*

Flashes of foresight bombard those fighting upon the battlefield, sudden squalls of prophecy and storms of foretelling showing them when and where to strike at their foes. Those closest bound to the warp benefit greatest of all, gaining godlike insight of the skeins of fate.

You can re-roll hit rolls of 1. You can instead re-roll failed hit rolls made for **Daemons** or **Psykers**.

43 EMPYRIC FEEDBACK — *Instantaneous*

A keening shriek begins to build across the battlefield, a screaming empyric gale that howls louder and more savagely by the moment. Psykers drop to their knees, hands clutched to their ears, tear ducts weeping blood, as the malefic screams reach an unbearable pitch.

Roll a dice for each **Psyker** on the battlefield: on a 4+ that model immediately suffers a mortal wound.

44 CONDUIT OF THE IMMATERIUM — *Instantaneous*

Like lightning striking a tree, a spike of warp energy earths itself through one of the psykers battling here. Knowing that to let that power ground within them is to invite an agonising death, the psyker desperately channels the sudden surge of power and unleashes it.

Randomly select a **Psyker** on the battlefield. That **Psyker** immediately manifests a psychic power it knows as if it were its Psychic phase. No Psychic test is necessary and no attempt to Deny the Witch can be made. After resolving the psychic power, the **Psyker** suffers Perils of the Warp.

45 WARP RESURRECTION — *Instantaneous*

With the warp in wild flux all around, the natural order of reality is perverted. The ghosts of the recently slain slither from the cold grip of death and flow back into their abandoned bodies, reknitting flesh and bone to rise and do battle once more.

Select one of your **Infantry** units that is on the battlefield: you can immediately return one slain model to that unit. You can instead return D3 slain models if the unit chosen has the Troops Battlefield Role.

46 EMPYRIC MASTERY — *Persistent*

The battlefield resides at the eye of the storm, an island of calm empyric currents amongst the madness of the maelstrom. Psykers find themselves able to control their powers – and to unmake those of the foe – with greater ease than they have ever known in their lives.

Re-roll failed Psychic tests and Deny the Witch tests.

51 OVERWHELMING POWER — *Persistent*

From amidst the seething madness of the warp storms, a meteoric blast of power roars down to strike one of the psykers upon the field of battle. Blazing with energy and potential, the suddenly energised warrior begins a rampage through the enemy forces.

Randomly select a **Psyker** on the battlefield. Double that model's Strength, Toughness and Attacks characteristics.

52 THE WARP BECALMED — *Persistent*

The warp storm dissipates as suddenly as it roared into being, vanishing so completely that – for a brief and blessed moment – the dangers of psychic predation vanish completely. The warring psykers seize their chance to wield their powers safely, knowing that such a blessing cannot last.

Psykers cannot suffer Perils of the Warp.

53 PSYCHIC DEVASTATION — *Persistent*

Clouds of psychic energy roll low over the battlefield, and disembodied eyes the size of spacecraft appear in the sky. Wherever psychic energies are unleashed in the shadow of this warp storm, their effects are vastly magnified.

Each time a psychic power is manifested and not resisted by a Deny the Witch test, resolve its effects, then resolve its effects again. If the psychic power allows you to target a unit, you can choose to select a different target for the second set of effects, or you can inflict double the damage, bestow twice the bonuses or inflict twice the penalties on the same unit. No additional Psychic test is required, and no Deny the Witch test can be taken to attempt to nullify the second set of effects.

54 EMPYRIC INVULNERABILITY — *Persistent*

Warp winds howl down in a tight, spiralling mass of dark energy and lashing, ectoplasmic tentacles, engulfing a psyker and warding away the blades, bolts and energy blasts of their enemies.

Randomly select a **Psyker** on the battlefield. Re-roll failed saves for that model.

55 UNCONTROLLED MUTATION — *Instantaneous*

As the tides of the warp surge higher, the energies they unleash begin to overwhelm the psykers on the battlefield. Flesh runs like candle wax. Tentacles, eyes and yawning maws tear through bone, and the screaming psyker degenerates into a bloated Spawn.

Randomly select a **Psyker** on the battlefield and roll 2D6: if the result is equal to or greater than that model's Leadership characteristic, it is slain and transformed into a Chaos Spawn. Before removing that psyker as a casualty, both players roll off. Whoever wins the roll-off takes control of the Chaos Spawn for the rest of the battle and sets it up anywhere within 6" of the psyker and more than 1" from any enemy models.

56 DARK POSSESSION — *Instantaneous*

Upon the screaming winds of the warp storm, an insidious voices hisses and beguiles, threatens and curses. Should one of the psykers upon the field of battle prove too weak-willed to resist its call, the Daemon approaching through the storm will steal their flesh for its own…

Randomly select a **Psyker** on the battlefield and roll 2D6: if the result is equal to or greater than that model's Leadership characteristic, it is slain and transformed into a Daemon Prince of Chaos. Before removing that psyker as a casualty, the player whose psyker was slain takes control of the Daemon Prince for the rest of the battle and sets it up anywhere within 6" of the psyker and more than 1" from any enemy models.

61 TERRORS OF THE WARP — *Persistent*

With the warp storm raging more furiously by the moment, predatory abominations from the empyric depths draw near to the battlefield. Their tendrils wind around the minds and souls of their prey, while their fangs gnash in anticipation of the feast.

Each time a **Psyker** suffers Perils of the Warp, it suffers D6 mortal wounds instead of D3.

62 WARP BLAST — *Instantaneous*

The sky above the battlefield fills with racing clouds of black smoke and flaring green lightning. Arcing bolts of warp energy leap down to flay the battlefield, blasting warriors to atoms and melting war engines into slag.

Roll a dice for each unit on the battlefield. On a 1 that unit suffers D3 mortal wounds.

63 UNREALITY REIGNS — *Persistent*

Time stutters and blinks. Gravity fluctuates, and the immutable laws of physics unravel to leave warriors flailing wildly, reeling in bewildered incomprehension.

All dice rolls of 1 count as 6, and all dice rolls of 6 count as 1.

64 PSYCHIC STUN — *Instantaneous*

The warp storm is lit by a sudden flash of blinding light. Those with psychic sensitivity look desperately away, attempting to shield their senses from the overwhelming blast of light and sound.

Roll a dice for each **Psyker** on the battlefield: on a 6 that **Psyker** immediately loses one randomly selected psychic power it knows. It cannot use this psychic power for the rest of the battle.

65 DAEMONTIDE — *Instantaneous*

As the warp storm rages across the battlefield, reality tears open with a terrible ripping sound, and a tide of unnatural entities spills through.

Both players roll off and whoever wins adds one unit of the following to their army and sets it up anywhere on the battlefield that is more than 9" from any enemy models: 10 Bloodletters, 10 Pink Horrors, 10 Plaguebearers or 10 Daemonettes.

66 EMPYRIC BREACH — *Instantaneous*

The catastrophic power of the warp storm surges, and a mighty rent in the empyrean opens upon the field of battle. Through the breach steps a mighty daemonic lord, an entity of cruelty and destruction that emits a triumphant roar of freedom before wading into the fight.

Both players roll off and whoever wins adds one of the following to their army and sets it up anywhere on the battlefield that is more than 9" from any enemy models: Bloodthirster of Unfettered Fury, Bloodthirster of Insensate Rage, Wrath of Khorne Bloodthirster, Lord of Change, Great Unclean One or Keeper of Secrets.

LADDER CAMPAIGNS

A brilliantly simple yet highly enjoyable campaign structure, the tried and tested ladder campaign will let you settle old rivalries and make brand new ones – all in the name of friendly competition, of course! Here you'll learn how to fight your way to the top, one rung at a time.

A great way to put your matched play army through its paces is to take part in a ladder campaign. These campaigns are easy to set up and versatile to play, making them ideal for gaming groups and school leagues. With straightforward rules, ladder campaigns are the perfect forum in which to trial your matched play army for the first time – although they are also ideal for seasoned players seeking to prove their worth in the crucible of battle.

In its simplest form, a ladder campaign involves participants attempting to battle their way to the top of the 'ladder' by defeating their fellows in games of Warhammer 40,000. The more battles a player wins, the higher up the ladder they will climb.

The concept sounds simple, but there can be a great deal of strategy involved. Pick your opponents wisely, as your next battle might propel you into top position – or send you right to the bottom! The trickiest part about scaling the ladder's giddy heights is staying at the top. The champion's position is the most precarious, as every other player will be vying to depose them.

You can use any of the rules presented in this and other Warhammer 40,000 publications when fighting your battles, but ladder campaigns are particularly well-suited to matched play gaming. Simply choose which matched play system you'd like to use and ensure that all participants follow it when putting together their armies. On the opposite page you will find an example ladder campaign that you can follow – or use as inspiration for creating your own – as well as some hints and tips for making your campaigns even more exciting and memorable.

LADDER OF COMMAND

A Warhammer 40,000 ladder campaign is a great way to organise a simple game league at a club. Players challenge each other in battle with the view of climbing the ladder, and whoever is at the top is considered the current reigning champion.

The concept of a ladder campaign is really very simple. A list of all of the players taking part is kept, with the first player to join being number one, the second player to join number two and so on. As new players join the ladder, they add their name to the end of the list and take the next number.

So a ladder with six players would have a list of six names numbered from one to six. If two players later joined the ladder, they would be given positions seven and eight, and so on.

When players in the ladder fight a battle, the result will affect their position on the ladder as described in the rules that follow. To play a ladder game, all you need to do is choose a willing opponent from the ladder, and arrange to fight a battle!

THE MISSION

The players choose which matched play mission they will play. This can be one found in this book, in the *Warhammer 40,000* rulebook, or in any other Warhammer 40,000 publication. Roll off if each player wishes to play a different mission – the winner can choose which mission is used.

THE ARMIES

We suggest that each player selects a Battle-forged army to an agreed points limit.

THE BATTLEFIELD

Create the battlefield, set up terrain and set up any objective markers that may be required, as described in the mission you are using.

DEPLOYMENT

The players set up their armies by following the instructions in the mission they are using.

VICTORY CONDITIONS

Determine the winner as described in the Victory Conditions section of the mission being used.

CLIMBING THE LADDER

If the winner of a battle is the lower of the two players on the ladder, they swap places with their opponent. If the winner is higher up the ladder, they swap places with the player that is directly above them, unless they are at the very top, in which case the loser drops a rung on the ladder. In the case of a tie, the players remain in their current positions. For example, if player five defeats player three in battle, they swap places. But if player three is victorious over player five, player three swaps places with player two.

In addition to the above, anyone who doesn't play a game for a month drops to the bottom of the ladder, falling below any players who have played games in the last month. The player at the top of the ladder is the current reigning champion!

UPDATED POINTS VALUES: DECEMBER 2017

Whenever we publish a new edition of *Chapter Approved*, or a new codex, we review, update and fine-tune the points values of all our datasheets. This means that the points values for the units and items of wargear that appear in one of the tables below replace those that appear in books with an earlier publication date, and also take precedence over points-value lists that have no publication date at all. If a unit or item of wargear does not appear in any of the tables below, continue to use the points values for it that are listed within the most recently published book for that Faction.

Note that sometimes a weapon can appear in several different books, each with different points costs (for example, power fists appear in both *Codex: Space Marines* and *Codex: Astra Militarum*). If such an item of wargear appears in one of the tables below, only apply the change to the appropriate Faction.

SPACE MARINES UNITS

UNIT	MODELS PER UNIT	POINTS PER MODEL (Does not include wargear)
Aggressor Squad	3-6	21
Chaplain in Terminator Armour	1	100
Drop Pod	1	83
Inceptor Squad	3-6	25
Intercessor Squad	5-10	18
Librarian	1	88
Librarian in Terminator Armour	1	120
Librarian with Jump Pack	1	112
Razorback	1	70
Stalker	1	75
Stormraven Gunship	1	192
Tartaros Terminator Squad	5-10	26
Terminator Assault Squad	5-10	26
Terminus Ultra	1	250
Vindicator	1	125
Whirlwind	1	70

SPACE MARINES WARGEAR

WARGEAR	POINTS PER ITEM
Assault bolter	10
Assault cannon	22
Assault plasma incinerator	17
Auto boltstorm gauntlets	12
Auxiliary grenade launcher	1
Boltstorm gauntlet	22
Centurion assault launchers	3
Force axe	10
Force stave	8
Force sword	8
Hurricane bolter	10
Ironclad assault launchers	5
Plasma exterminator	17
Predator autocannon	40
Twin assault cannon	44

SPACE MARINES NAMED CHARACTERS

UNIT	MODELS PER UNIT	POINTS PER MODEL (Including wargear)
Roboute Guilliman	1	385
Sergeant Chronus	1	40

GREY KNIGHTS UNITS

UNIT	MODELS PER UNIT	POINTS PER MODEL (Does not include wargear)
Razorback	1	70
Stormraven Gunship	1	192
Terminator Squad	5-10	41

GREY KNIGHTS WARGEAR

WARGEAR	POINTS PER ITEM
Assault cannon	22
Hurricane bolter	10
Twin assault cannon	44

ADEPTUS MINISTORUM UNITS

UNIT	MODELS PER UNIT	POINTS PER MODEL (Does not include wargear)
Exorcist	1	135

ADEPTUS MINISTORUM NAMED CHARACTERS

UNIT	MODELS PER UNIT	POINTS PER MODEL (Including wargear)
Celestine	1	200
- Geminae Superia	0-2	25

ADEPTUS MINISTORUM WARGEAR

WARGEAR	POINTS PER ITEM
Eviscerator	12
Hand flamer	3
Inferno pistol	9
Storm bolter	2

ADEPTUS MECHANICUS UNITS

UNIT	MODELS PER UNIT	POINTS PER MODEL (Does not include wargear)
Fulgurite Electro-Priests	5-20	16
Kataphron Breachers	3-12	30
Kataphron Destroyers	3-12	30
Sicarian Infiltrators	5-10	16
Skitarii Rangers	5-10	7
Skitarii Vanguard	5-10	8
Tech-Priest Dominus	1	115
Tech-Priest Enginseer	1	35

ADEPTUS MECHANICUS NAMED CHARACTERS

UNIT	MODELS PER UNIT	POINTS PER MODEL (Including wargear)
Belisarius Cawl	1	240

ADEPTUS MECHANICUS WARGEAR

WARGEAR	POINTS PER ITEM
Enhanced data-tether	5
Eradication beamer	25
Eradication ray	10
Heavy arc rifle	6
Phosphor blast pistol	3
Phosphor blaster	6
Phosphor serpenta	4
Power fist	12
Radium pistol	0
Taser goad	4
Torsion cannon	20

DEATHWATCH UNITS

UNIT	MODELS PER UNIT	POINTS PER MODEL (Does not include wargear)
Aggressor Squad	3-6	21
Drop Pod	1	83
Hellblaster Squad	5-10	18
Inceptor Squad	3-6	25
Intercessor Squad	5-10	18
Librarian	1	88
Librarian with Jump Pack	1	112
Razorback	1	70

DEATHWATCH WARGEAR

WARGEAR	POINTS PER ITEM
Assault bolter	10
Assault cannon	22
Assault plasma incinerator	17
Auto boltstorm gauntlets	12
Auxiliary grenade launcher	1
Boltstorm gauntlet	22
Force axe	10
Force stave	8
Force sword	8
Hurricane bolter	10
Lightning claws (single/pair)	8/12
Plasma exterminator	17
Power fist	12
Storm shield (CHARACTERS)	15
Storm shield (other models)	5
Thunder hammer (CHARACTERS)	21
Thunder hammer (other models)	16
Twin assault cannon	44

SPACE WOLVES UNITS

UNIT	MODELS PER UNIT	POINTS PER MODEL (Does not include wargear)
Aggressor Squad	3-6	21
Bjorn the Fell-Handed	1	200
Drop Pod	1	83
Fenrisian Wolves	5-15	6 (Cyberwolf is 15)
Grey Hunters	5-10	13
Hellblaster Squad	5-10	18
Inceptor Squad	3-6	25
Intercessor Squad	5-10	18
Long Fangs	5-6	14
Razorback	1	70
Rune Priest	1	88
Rune Priest with Jump Pack	1	112
Stormfang Gunship	1	175
Swiftclaws	3-9	23 (Swiftclaw Attack Bike is 35)
Thunderwolf Cavalry	3-6	40
Vindicator	1	125
Whirlwind	1	70
Wolf Guard Battle Leader in Terminator Armour	1	91
Wolf Guard Battle Leader on Thunderwolf	1	94
Wolf Guard in Terminator Armour	5-10	26
Wolf Guard Pack Leader in Terminator Armour	N/A	26
Wolf Guard with Jump Packs	5-10	19
Wolf Lord on Thunderwolf	1	108
Wolf Priest	1	75
Wolf Priest in Terminator Armour	1	105
Wolf Priest with Jump Pack	1	97
Wulfen	5-10	28

SPACE WOLVES NAMED CHARACTERS

UNIT	MODELS PER UNIT	POINTS PER MODEL (Including wargear)
Arjac Rockfist	1	145
Canis Wolfborn	1	125
Krom Dragongaze	1	115
Murderfang	1	170
Njal Stormcaller in Terminator Armour	1	153
Ragnar Blackmane	1	141
- Svangir and Ulfgir	2	6
Ulrik the Slayer	1	110

SPACE WOLVES WARGEAR

WARGEAR	POINTS PER ITEM
Assault bolter	10
Assault cannon	22
Assault plasma incinerator	17
Auto boltstorm gauntlets	12
Auxiliary grenade launcher	1
Blizzard shield	30
Boltstorm gauntlet	22
Hurricane bolter	10
Plasma exterminator	17
Power fist	12
Predator autocannon	40
Psychic hood	5
Runic axe	12
Runic stave	10
Runic sword	10
Storm shield (CHARACTERS)	15
Storm shield (Thunderwolf Cavalry)	10
Storm shield (other models)	5
Thunder hammer (CHARACTERS)	21
Thunder hammer (other models)	16
Twin assault cannon	44
Wolf claw (single/pair)	10/14

ASTRA MILITARUM UNITS

UNIT	MODELS PER UNIT	POINTS PER MODEL (Does not include wargear)
Astropath	1	30
Conscripts	20-30	4
Manticore	1	135
Primaris Psyker	1	38
Ratlings	5-10	7
Taurox	1	50
Taurox Prime	1	80
Wyverns	1-3	95

ASTRA MILITARUM WARGEAR

WARGEAR	POINTS PER ITEM
Autocannon	12
Force stave	8
Hot-shot volley gun	7
Meltagun (model with a Ballistic Skill of 4+)	12
Meltagun (other models)	17
Power fist	8
Taurox gatling cannon	20
Tempestus command rod	5
Vanquisher battle cannon	20

DEATH GUARD UNITS

UNIT	MODELS PER UNIT	POINTS PER MODEL (Does not include wargear)
Deathshroud Terminators	3-6	35
Defiler	1	140
Lord of Contagion	1	100
Noxious Blightbringer	1	58
Plague Marines	5-20	17
Plagueburst Crawler	1	100
Sorcerer in Terminator Armour	1	120
Tallyman	1	55

DEATH GUARD WARGEAR

WARGEAR	POINTS PER ITEM
Blight launcher	10
Force axe	10
Force stave	8
Force sword	8
Helbrute fist (single/pair)	40/50
Predator autocannon	40

CHAOS SPACE MARINES UNITS

UNIT	MODELS PER UNIT	POINTS PER MODEL (Does not include wargear)
Chaos Bikers	3-9	23
Chaos Vindicator	1	125
Defiler	1	140
Horrors	10-30	
- Blue Horrors		5
- Pairs of Brimstone Horrors		3
- Pink Horrors		7
Khorne Lord of Skulls	1	380
Mutilators	3	42
Plague Marines	5-20	17
Sorcerer in Terminator Armour	1	120
Sorcerer with Jump Pack	1	112

CHAOS SPACE MARINES WARGEAR

WARGEAR	POINTS PER ITEM
Autocannon	15
Blight launcher	10
Bubotic axe	5
Chainfist	14
Doom siren	10
Force axe	10
Force stave	8
Force sword	8
Helbrute fist (single/pair)	40/50
Icon of Flame	5
Icon of Vengeance	5
Predator autocannon	40
Warp bolter	3

THOUSAND SONS UNITS

UNIT	MODELS PER UNIT	POINTS PER MODEL (Does not include wargear)
Exalted Sorcerer	1	112
Exalted Sorcerer on Disc of Tzeentch	1	146

CHAOS BASTION WARGEAR

WARGEAR	POINTS PER ITEM
Heavy bolter	8

HARLEQUINS UNITS

UNIT	MODELS PER UNIT	POINTS PER MODEL (Does not include wargear)
Death Jester	1	60

HARLEQUINS WARGEAR

WARGEAR	POINTS PER ITEM
Harlequin's caress	7
Harlequin's kiss	9

DRUKHARI UNITS

UNIT	MODELS PER UNIT	POINTS PER MODEL (Does not include wargear)
Lhamaean	1	18
Medusae	1	21
Razorwing Flock	3-12	14
Sslyth	1	31
Ur-Ghul	1	20

ORKS UNITS

UNIT	MODELS PER UNIT	POINTS PER MODEL (Does not include wargear)
Morkanaut	1	250
Skorchas	1-5	37
Warbuggies	1-5	33
Wartrakks	1-5	37

ORKS WARGEAR

WARGEAR	POINTS PER ITEM
Big choppa	7
Killkannon	15
Killsaw/two killsaws	15/23
Kombi-weapon with rokkit launcha	14
Kopta rokkits	24
Kustom mega-kannon	17
Power klaw	13
Rack of rokkits	24
Shokk attack gun	25
Twin big shoota	10

GENESTEALER CULTS UNITS

UNIT	MODELS PER UNIT	POINTS PER MODEL (Does not include wargear)
Purestrain Genestealers	5-20	15

GENESTEALER CULTS WARGEAR

WARGEAR	POINTS PER ITEM
Cult icon	20
Eradicator nova cannon	25
Heavy rock saw	14
Heavy seismic cannon	15
Power hammer	16
Power maul	4
Power pick	10
Purestrain talons	0
Seismic cannon	10
Vanquisher battle cannon	20

UPDATED POINTS VALUES: FORGE WORLD

As part of our update of point values, we have also reviewed Forge World's range of units. The points values for the units and items of wargear that appear in one of the tables below replace those that appear in books with an earlier publication date, and also take precedence over points-value lists that have no publication date at all. If a unit or item of wargear does not appear in any of the tables below, continue to use the points values for it that are listed within the most recently published datasheet for that Faction.

ADEPTUS ASTARTES UNITS

UNIT	MODELS PER UNIT	POINTS PER MODEL (Does not include wargear)
Caestus Assault Ram	1	250
Deimos Relic Predator	1	90
Fire Raptor Gunship	1	190
Infernum Pattern Razorback	1	70
Land Speeder Tempest	1-3	95
Lucius Dreadnought Drop Pod	1	80
Relic Cerberus Heavy Tank Destroyer	1	680
Relic Falchion Super-Heavy Tank	1	840
Relic Fellblade Super-Heavy Tank	1	740
Relic Javelin Attack Speeder	1	110
Relic Mastodon Super-Heavy Transport	1	934
Relic Sicaran	1	155
Relic Sicaran Punisher	1	155
Relic Sicaran Venator	1	170
Relic Typhon Heavy Siege Tank	1	720
Siege Dreadnought	1	80
Sokar Pattern Stormbird	1	2000
Tarantula Air Defence Battery	1-3	70
Tarantula Sentry Gun	1-3	20
Thunderhawk Gunship	1	1330
Thunderhawk Transporter	1	1000
Xiphon Interceptor	1	110

ADEPTUS ASTARTES WARGEAR

WARGEAR	POINTS PER ITEM
Assault cannon	22
Cyclone missile launcher	50
Dreadnought chainfist (single/pair)	46/56
Dreadnought combat weapon (single/pair)	40/50
Grav-flux bombard	65
Leviathan siege claw (single/pair)	55/65
Leviathan siege drill (single/pair)	65/75
Power fist	12
Predator autocannon	40
Punisher rotary cannon	0
Twin accelerator autocannon	0
Twin assault cannon	44
Twin autocannon	30

GREY KNIGHTS, INQUISITION & SISTERS OF BATTLE UNITS

UNIT	MODELS PER UNIT	POINTS PER MODEL (Does not include wargear)
Vortimer Pattern Razorback	1	70
Thunderhawk Assault Gunship	1	1130
Sororitas Repressor	1	91

GREY KNIGHTS, INQUISITION & SISTERS OF BATTLE WARGEAR

WARGEAR	POINTS PER ITEM
Twin psycannon	50

DAEMON BOUND UNITS

UNIT	MODELS PER UNIT	POINTS PER MODEL (Does not include wargear)
Greater Blight Drone	1	170
Greater Brass Scorpion of Khorne	1	650

DAEMON BOUND WARGEAR

WARGEAR	POINTS PER ITEM
Butcher cannon	30
Soulburner petard	60

HELLFORGED UNITS

UNIT	MODELS PER UNIT	POINTS PER MODEL (Does not include wargear)
Chaos Space Marine Crew	N/A	10
Hellforged Cerberus Heavy Destroyer	1	650
Hellforged Contemptor Dreadnought	1	103
Hellforged Dreadclaw Drop Pod	1	130
Hellforged Falchion	1	840
Hellforged Fellblade	1	740
Hellforged Kharybdis Assault Claw	1	375
Hellforged Mastodon	1	934
Hellforged Predator	1	95
Hellforged Sicaran Venator	1	175
Hellforged Typhon Heavy Siege Tank	1	700

HELLFORGED WARGEAR

WARGEAR	POINTS PER ITEM
Butcher cannon	30
Butcher cannon array	60
Dual malignatas saker	50
Hellforged chainclaw (single/pair)	45/55
Hellforged siege claw (single/pair)	55/65
Hellforged siege drill (single/pair)	65/75
Magna-melta cannon	70
Malignatas beam laser	0
Predator autocannon	40
Soulburner	30
Soulburner bombard	90
Twin accelerator autocannon	0

EYRINE CULTS UNITS

UNIT	MODELS PER UNIT	POINTS PER MODEL (Does not include wargear)
Chaos Fire Raptor Assault Gunship	1	190
Chaos Hell Talon	1	180
Chaos Sokar Pattern Stormbird Gunship	1	2000
Chaos Thunderhawk Assault Gunship	1	1330
Chaos Xiphon Interceptor	1	110

EYRINE CULTS WARGEAR

WARGEAR	POINTS PER ITEM
Balefire missiles	30
Reaper battery	30

LORDS OF RUIN UNITS

UNIT	MODELS PER UNIT	POINTS PER MODEL (Does not include wargear)
Zhufor the Impaler*	1	130

LORDS OF RUIN WARGEAR

WARGEAR	POINTS PER ITEM
Soulburner pistol	20
Infernal axe	8

CHILDREN OF THE WARP UNITS

UNIT	MODELS PER UNIT	POINTS PER MODEL (Does not include wargear)
Aetaos'rau'keres*	1	1500
An'ggrath the Unbound*	1	888
Giant Chaos Spawn	1	150
Mamon Transfigured*	1	220
Plague Toads of Nurgle	3-9	58
Pox Riders of Nurgle	3-9	63
Samus*	1	170
Scabeiathrax the Bloated*	1	777
Spined Chaos Beast	1	150
Uraka the Warfiend*	1	150
Zarakynel*	1	666

CHILDREN OF THE WARP WARGEAR

WARGEAR	POINTS PER ITEM
Daemonic Icon	15

TRAITOR QUESTORIS UNITS

UNIT	MODELS PER UNIT	POINTS PER MODEL (Does not include wargear)
Renegade Knight Porphyrion	1	600

HERETIC TITAN LEGIONS UNITS

UNIT	MODELS PER UNIT	POINTS PER MODEL (Does not include wargear)
Chaos Reaver Battle Titan	1	4000
Chaos Warhound Scout Titan	1	2000
Chaos Warlord Battle Titan	1	6000

ASTRA MILITARUM UNITS

UNIT	MODELS PER UNIT	POINTS PER MODEL (Does not include wargear)
Armageddon Pattern Medusa	1-3	115
Artemia Pattern Hellhound	1-3	73
Avenger Strike Fighter	1	150
Cyclops Demolition Vehicle	1-3	60
Dominus Armoured Siege Bombard	1	600
Earthshaker Battery	1-3	115
Earthshaker Carriage Battery		
- Earthshaker Carriage	1-3	105
- Guardsman Crewman	4-12	4
Gorgon Heavy Transporter	1	300
Griffon Mortar Carrier	1-3	77

* There may only be a single unit of this type in any given army.

ASTRA MILITARUM UNITS CONT.

UNIT	MODELS PER UNIT	POINTS PER MODEL (Does not include wargear)
Heavy Quad Launcher Battery		
- Heavy Quad Launcher	1-3	85
- Guardsman Crew	3-9	4
Hydra Battery	1-3	75
Imperial Fortress Walls	1	800
Leman Russ Annihilator	1-3	122
Leman Russ Conqueror	1-3	122
Leman Russ Stygies Vanquisher	1-3	160
Lightning Strike Fighter	1	125
Manticore Battery	1-3	110
Medusa Carriage Battery		
- Medusa Carriage	1-3	100
- Guardsmen Crew	4-12	4
Primaris Redoubt	1	700
Rapier Laser Destroyer		
- Rapier Laser Destroyer	1	80
- Guardsmen Crew	2	4
Salamander Command Vehicle	1	110
Stygies Destroyer Tank Hunter	1-3	160
Stygies Thunderer Siege Tank	1-3	160
Tarantula Battery	1-3	20
Thunderbolt Heavy Fighter	1	125

ASTRA MILITARUM WARGEAR

WARGEAR	POINTS PER ITEM
Autocannon	12
Defence searchlight	20
Hellstrike missile	30
Meltagun (model with a Ballistic Skill of 4+)	12
Meltagun (other models)	17
Plasma gun (models with a Ballistic Skill of 4+)	7
Plasma gun (other models)	13
Power fist	8
Twin assault cannon	44

DEATH KORPS OF KRIEG UNITS

UNIT	MODELS PER UNIT	POINTS PER MODEL (Does not include wargear)
Death Korps of Krieg Command Squad**	4	7
Death Korps Combat Engineer Squad**	5-10	7
Death Korps Grenadier Storm Squad**	5-10	8
Death Korps Leman Russ Mars Alpha Battle Tanks	1-3	122

DEATH KORPS OF KRIEG WARGEAR

WARGEAR	POINTS PER ITEM
Autocannon	12
Meltagun (model with a Ballistic Skill of 4+)	12
Meltagun (other models)	17
Plasma gun (models with a Ballistic Skill of 4+)	7
Plasma gun (other models)	13
Power fist	8
Storm armour and mine plough	10
Twin heavy stubber	8
Vanquisher battle cannon	20

ELYSIAN DROP TROOPS UNITS

UNIT	MODELS PER UNIT	POINTS PER MODEL (Does not include wargear)
Elysian Command Squad**	4	7
Elysian Veteran Squad**	10	7

ELYSIAN DROP TROOPS WARGEAR

WARGEAR	POINTS PER ITEM
Meltagun (model with a Ballistic Skill of 4+)	12
Meltagun (other models)	17
Plasma gun (model with a Ballistic Skill of 4+)	7
Plasma gun (other models)	13
Power fist	8

RENEGADES AND HERETICS UNITS

UNIT	MODELS PER UNIT	POINTS PER MODEL (Does not include wargear)
Malefic Lord	1	80
Renegade Command Squad**	4-14	6
Renegade Disciple Squad**	5-15	6
Renegade Militia Squad**	10-20	4
Renegade Cultists	10-30	4

RENEGADES AND HERETICS WARGEAR

WARGEAR	POINTS PER ITEM
Autocannon	12
Meltagun (model with a Ballistic Skill of 4+)	12
Meltagun (other models)	17
Plasma gun (models with a Ballistic Skill of 4+)	7
Plasma gun (other models)	13
Power fist	8

** If models in these units form Heavy Weapons Teams, there is no additional points cost.

QUESTOR IMPERIALIS UNITS

UNIT	MODELS PER UNIT	POINTS PER MODEL (Does not include wargear)
Acastus Knight Porphyrion	1	600

TITAN LEGIONS UNITS

UNIT	MODELS PER UNIT	POINTS PER MODEL (Does not include wargear)
Reaver Battle Titan	1	4000
Warhound Scout Titan	1	2000
Warlord Battle Titan	1	6000

NECRONS UNITS

UNIT	MODELS PER UNIT	POINTS PER MODEL (Does not include wargear)
Gauss Pylon	1	550
Night Shroud	1	220

TYRANIDS UNITS

UNIT	MODELS PER UNIT	POINTS PER MODEL (Does not include wargear)
Barbed Hierodule	1	420
Hierophant Bio-titan	1	2000
Malanthrope	1-3	140

TYRANIDS WARGEAR

WARGEAR	POINTS PER ITEM
Massive scything talons (one pair)	22
Massive scything talons (two or more pairs)	60

ORKS UNITS

UNIT	MODELS PER UNIT	POINTS PER MODEL (Does not include wargear)
'Chinork' Warkopta	1	74
Kill Tank	1	365
Squiggoth	1	160

ORKS WARGEAR

WARGEAR	POINTS PER ITEM
Killkannon	15
Lifta-droppa	0
Rack of rokkits	24
Twin big shoota	10
Supa-kannon	30
Big choppa	7

DRUKHARI UNITS

UNIT	MODELS PER UNIT	POINTS PER MODEL (Does not include wargear)
Tantalus	1	400

T'AU EMPIRE UNITS

UNIT	MODELS PER UNIT	POINTS PER MODEL (Does not include wargear)
Blacklight Marker Drones	N/A	7
TX7 Heavy Bombardment Hammerhead Gunship	1	117
TX7 Fire Support Hammerhead Gunship	1	117
Manta Super-heavy Dropship	1	2000
KX139 Ta'unar Supremacy Armour	1	1500

ASURYANI UNITS

UNIT	MODELS PER UNIT	POINTS PER MODEL (Does not include wargear)
Corsair Cloud Dancer Band	3-9	20
- Corsair Cloud Dancer Felarch	0-1	25
Corsair Reaver Band	5-15	7
- Corsair Reaver Felarch	0-1	12
Corsair Skyreaver Band	5-10	10
- Corsair Skyreaver Felarch	0-1	15
Phoenix	1	183
Revenant Titan	1	2000
Scorpion	1	700
Vampire Hunter	1	1500
Warp Hunter	1	285
Wasp Assault Walker	1-3	65
Wraithseer	1	125

ASURYANI WARGEAR

WARGEAR	POINTS PER ITEM
D-cannon	45
Deathshroud cannon	45
Prism blaster	30
Prism rifle	25
Scatter laser	10
Shuriken cannon	10
Sonic lance	60
Starcannon	15
Twin shuriken catapult	5
Twin shuriken cannon	17
Twin starcannon	28

BATTLE-FORGED ARMIES

When picking a Battle-forged army for matched play, you will need to record the details of your army on a piece of paper (your Army Roster). Here we show one example of how you can do this, using several Detachment Rosters – at least one for each Detachment in your army – and one main Army Roster as a summary. Over the page are blank rosters you can photocopy.

DETACHMENT ROSTERS

Each Detachment Roster details all the units a Detachment includes. Each unit section has room for you to write down the name and type of the unit, its Battlefield Role, the number of models it contains, and the wargear each model is equipped with. Details of how many models make up each unit and what weapons and upgrades each can take can be found on that unit's datasheet.

The points values of each unit's models and each individual weapon is then calculated by referencing the points values in the appropriate codex, and then added together to give a points cost for the unit. The points value of the entire Detachment is simply the sum of the points values of its units. This can be noted down alongside other useful information, such as the number of Command Points (if any) the Detachment gives you (see the *Warhammer 40,000* rulebook for more on Command Points).

Unit Champions

Many units are led by a champion of some kind such as a Sergeant. Unit champions often have better characteristics and weapon options. Unless noted otherwise, unit champions have the same points cost as the other models in their unit.

Under-strength Units

Sometimes you may find that you do not have enough models to field a minimum-sized unit; if this is the case, you can still include one unit of that type in your army, with as many models as you have available. An under-strength unit still takes up the appropiate slot in a Detachment. In matched play games, you can only include under-strength units in Auxiliary Support Detachments, but you only pay the points for the models you actually have (and any wargear they are equipped with).

ARMY ROSTER

Once you have filled in all of your Detachment Rosters, you can then fill out the main Army Roster. The name and points value of each Detachment is noted down here for reference. The total points value of your army is the sum of all the Detachment points values in your army plus any reinforcement points you have chosen to put aside (see below). The points value of your army should not exceed the points limit you are using for the battle.

There are lots of other useful things to write down on your main Army Roster, such as who the army's Warlord is (this should be done at the start of the battle) and the number of Command Points available to your army. Remember that all Battle-forged armies start with 3 Command Points, but certain Detachments, and occasionally certain models, can change this total.

Reinforcement Points

Sometimes an ability will allow you to add units to your army, or replace units that have been destroyed. You must set aside some of your points in order to use these units and record them on your army roster; these are your reinforcement points. Each time a unit is added to an army during battle, subtract the number of points the unit would cost from your pool of reinforcement points.

ARMY ROSTER

PLAYER NAME:	Alex Smith	ARMY FACTION:	Adeptus Astartes
ARMY NAME:	Strike Force Calgar	WARLORD:	Marneus Calgar

DETACHMENT NAME	TYPE	CPS	POINTS
Lords of Macragge	Patrol	0+2	657
4th Battle Demi-company	Battalion	3	931
Ultima Task Force	Vanguard	1	412

WARLORD TRAIT		
FILL IN AT SET-UP:		

Total Command Points:	9
Reinforcement Points:	0
TOTAL POINTS:	2000

DETACHMENT ROSTER

NAME:	Lords of Macragge	TYPE:	Patrol

UNIT

UNIT TITLE:	BATTLEFIELD ROLE:	NO. OF MODELS:	POINTS (MODELS):
Marneus Calgar	HQ	1	200

WARGEAR:	POINTS (WARGEAR):
Gauntlets of Ultramar and relic blade (all wargear points included in the model's points)	N/A

	TOTAL POINTS (UNIT):
	200

UNIT

UNIT TITLE:	BATTLEFIELD ROLE:	NO. OF MODELS:	POINTS (MODELS):
Tactical Squad	Troops	10	130

WARGEAR:	POINTS (WARGEAR):
Chainsword (0), missile launcher (25), plasma gun (13), 7 x boltguns (0), 10 x bolt pistols (0), 10 x frag and krak grenades (0)	38

	TOTAL POINTS (UNIT):
	168

UNIT

UNIT TITLE:	BATTLEFIELD ROLE:	NO. OF MODELS:	POINTS (MODELS):
Devastator Squad	Heavy Support	5	65

WARGEAR:	POINTS (WARGEAR):
Combi-plasma (15), 2 x heavy bolters (20), 2 x lascannon (50), 5 x bolt pistols (0), 5 x frag and krak grenades (0), Armorium Cherub (5)	90

	TOTAL POINTS (UNIT):
	155

UNIT

UNIT TITLE:	BATTLEFIELD ROLE:	NO. OF MODELS:	POINTS (MODELS):
Dreadnought	Elites	1	70

WARGEAR:	POINTS (WARGEAR):
Assault cannon (22), Dreadnought combat weapon (40), storm bolter (2)	64

	TOTAL POINTS (UNIT):
	134

Total Points (Detachment):	657	Command Points:	0+2

NOTES:	Detachment has Defenders of Humanity ability.
	All units are Ultramarines and so have Codex Discipline Chapter Tactic.
	Gain 2 Command Points if Marneus Calgar is the army's Warlord.

ARMY ROSTER

PLAYER NAME:

ARMY FACTION:

ARMY NAME:

WARLORD:

DETACHMENT NAME	TYPE	CPS	POINTS

WARLORD TRAIT

FILL IN AT SET-UP:

Total Command Points:	
Reinforcement Points:	
TOTAL POINTS:	

DETACHMENT ROSTER

NAME: | **TYPE:**

UNIT

UNIT TITLE:		BATTLEFIELD ROLE:	NO. OF MODELS:	POINTS (MODELS):
WARGEAR:				POINTS (WARGEAR):
			TOTAL POINTS (UNIT):	

UNIT

UNIT TITLE:		BATTLEFIELD ROLE:	NO. OF MODELS:	POINTS (MODELS):
WARGEAR:				POINTS (WARGEAR):
			TOTAL POINTS (UNIT):	

UNIT

UNIT TITLE:		BATTLEFIELD ROLE:	NO. OF MODELS:	POINTS (MODELS):
WARGEAR:				POINTS (WARGEAR):
			TOTAL POINTS (UNIT):	

UNIT

UNIT TITLE:		BATTLEFIELD ROLE:	NO. OF MODELS:	POINTS (MODELS):
WARGEAR:				POINTS (WARGEAR):
			TOTAL POINTS (UNIT):	

Total Points (Detachment): | **Command Points:**

NOTES:

30 POWER

NAME	M	WS	BS	S	T	W	A	Ld	Sv

DAMAGE

Some of this model's characteristics change as it suffers damage, as shown below:

REMAINING W	M	BS	A

WEAPON	RANGE	TYPE	S	AP	D	ABILITIES

WARGEAR OPTIONS

ABILITIES

TRANSPORT

FACTION KEYWORDS

KEYWORDS

OPEN PLAY